KU-452-255

‖‖‖‖‖‖‖‖‖‖‖‖‖‖‖‖‖‖‖‖‖‖‖

Overkill

The race to save Africa's wildlife

BY THE SAME AUTHOR

NATURAL HISTORY
Man is the Prey (London, New York 1968)
Focus on Fauna (Johannesburg 1970)
The Bushman (Johannesburg 1971)
Our Fragile Land (Johannesburg 1974)
The Environmental Crisis (Johannesburg 1974)
Bottero's Wildlife Art Collection (Johannesburg 1978)
Survival Guide to the Outdoors (Johannesburg 1987)
Mountain Odyssey (with David Coulson) (Cape Town 1983)
Roof of Africa (with David Coulson) (New York 1984)
Sabi Sabi (Johannesburg 1990)
Back to Earth (Cape Town 1991)
Coming back to Earth (Cape Town 2001)
Save Me from the Lion's Mouth (Cape Town 2012)

CULTURAL HISTORY
Like it Was (Johannesburg 1987)
An Extraordinary 20th Century (Johannesburg 1999)

ANTHOLOGIES
The Bedside Star (edited) (Johannesburg 1988)
Bedtime Again (edited) (Johannesburg 1990)
Back to Bed (edited) (Cape Town 1991)
Laugh, the Beloved Country (with Harvey Tyson) (Cape Town 2003)

HUMOUR
The Yellow Six (Birmingham and Johannesburg 1994 & 2006)
The Search for the Great South African Limerick (Johannesburg 1996)
S*x for the Extremely Shy (Johannesburg 1995)
Enclosed, Please Find (Johannesburg 1999)
Great South African Limericks (Johannesburg 1997)
Clarke on Your Stoep (Johannesburg 2005)
The Funny Side of Golf (Johannesburg 2005)

TRAVEL
Blazing Saddles – the Truth Behind the Tours de Farce. (Cape Town 2007)
Blazing Bicycle Saddles (Amazon/Kindle 2011)

Author's note: I have dispensed with footnotes as much as possible;
it is usually quicker to use keywords or names from the text
and follow up on the Internet.

Overkill

The race to save Africa's wildlife

James Clarke

Published by Struik Nature
(an imprint of Penguin Random House South Africa (Pty) Ltd)
Reg. No. 1953/000441/07
The Estuaries No. 4, Oxbow Crescent, Century City, 7441 South Africa
PO Box 1144, Cape Town, 8000 South Africa

Visit **www.penguinrandomhouse.co.za** and join the Struik Nature Club
for updates, news, events and special offers.

First published in 2017
1 3 5 7 9 10 8 6 4 2

Copyright © in text, 2017: James Clarke
Copyright © in map, 2017: Chris & Mathilde Stuart
Copyright © in published edition, 2017: Penguin Random House
South Africa (Pty) Ltd

Publisher: Pippa Parker
Editor: Charles de Villiers
Typesetter: Deirdré Geldenhuys
Proofreader and indexer: Thea Grobbelaar
Cover design: Michiel Botha
Cover images: Donovan van Staden/Shutterstock.com (elephant)
and Ana Gram/Shutterstock.com (birds)

Reproduction by Hirt & Carter Cape (Pty) Ltd
Printed and bound by Novus Print Solutions, Cape Town, South Africa

Printed by

All rights reserved. No part of this publication may be reproduced, stored in
a retrieval system, or transmitted, in any form or by any means, electronic,
mechanical, photocopying, recording, or otherwise, without the prior
permission of the copyright owners and publishers.

Print: 9781775845775
ePub: 9781775845782
ePDF: 9781775845799

Contents

What this book is about

Ninety per cent of the world's megafauna – its larger creatures – has disappeared since humans migrated from Africa and fanned out across Eurasia, and from there across the rest of the world. A picture is emerging of what happened when *Homo sapiens* crossed on to continents where humankind was unknown. Within a short time the megafauna – mammoths, mastodons, woolly rhinoceroses, as well as the huge carnivores that preyed upon them – were extinct. Not just a few species, but whole genera were wiped out.

The animals totally misjudged these strange little aliens and initially saw no reason to retreat from them. In fact, the humans were super-predators, and they triggered extinctions and massive habitat destruction across every continent and every island.

There was one exception: Africa itself.

Africa, the nursery from which *Homo sapiens* came, is the only landmass that today has most of its megafauna intact. The survivors of the Pleistocene still live across thousands of square kilometres of sub-Saharan Africa.

Overkill describes how this came about, and traces the history of human impact on land-based and marine megafauna. It examines the roles played by hunters, past and present, good and bad.

It describes how, in the 21st century, "big-game" populations in Africa began to lurch towards the edge of oblivion. By 2016, the African lion population had fallen to between

20,000 and 25,000. The elephant population fell by 100,000 in a few years. Rhinoceroses, which were saved from extinction 50 years ago, were being shot at the rate of three a day. The giraffe population plummeted to around 100,000.

Far Eastern nationals – residents, visitors and even diplomats – were implicated in this casual slaughter of protected species. Their depredations cost, annually, the deaths of tens of thousands of megafauna, marine and terrestrial. Every country south of the Sahara was pillaged, and 90% of the contraband was bound for China and Vietnam. This overkill rates as one of history's biggest international crimes.

After any war, and this has been a war, the aggressor is obliged to pay reparations. But will China, the prime aggressor, and its accomplices be held to account and forced to help fund the restoration of the areas they have ravaged?

In 2016, the African wildlife situation reached its lowest ebb.

The good news is this: the lowest ebb is always the turn of the tide.

Acknowledgements

Once again, I am hugely indebted to my two daughters: Julie Clarke-Havemann who, even as an overworked scientist concerned with environmental impact analyses in Africa, spent a lot of time helping with research and offering ideas, and Jenny Nourse, another busy person as a teaching biologist, who was so generous with her time and suggestions.

I am grateful to so many involved in conservation from South to East Africa that it's impossible to name them all, but special thanks to Alan Calenborne, Dr Jeremy Anderson – founder member of International Conservation Services (conserva@global.co.za), Peter Sullivan, Derek du Plessis, Harvey Tyson and all those former colleagues now in the top echelons of conservation journalism: Shree Bega (*The Star*), Tony Carnie (freelance, formerly *Daily News*), Ivo Vegter (*Daily Maverick*), Fiona McLeod (*Mail & Guardian*), Melanie Gosling (*Cape Times*), John Yeld (*Cape Argus*), Don Pinnock (*Daily Maverick*), Oscar Nkala (Botswana) and that most excellent of science writers, Shaun Smilie (*The Times; The Star*). Whenever I began to buckle under the avalanche of data I was always inspired by fellow sufferers of *cacoethes scribendi** – Richard Steyn, Gordon Forbes, Charles van Onselen, Peter Bruce, Mark Henning and the late Tim Couzens.

And I owe a lot to my dear companion, Mary Broadley, for her encouragement when it was needed most.

I also owe thanks to Charles de Villiers who stoically and patiently edited this book, a task made harder by the ever-changing scene in the war between those who were killing Africa's wildlife and those defending it.

And last, but far from least, I am ever grateful to that very patient soul, Pippa Parker, head of publishing at Struik Nature, for appreciating the significance of 2017 as a landmark in the unfolding drama of Africa's wildlife.

* the itch to write

Dedication

This book is dedicated to the memory of my lifelong friend, Ian Player (1927–2014), who heroically demonstrated that an endangered species – the white rhino – can be brought back from the brink.

Game and nature reserves of Africa

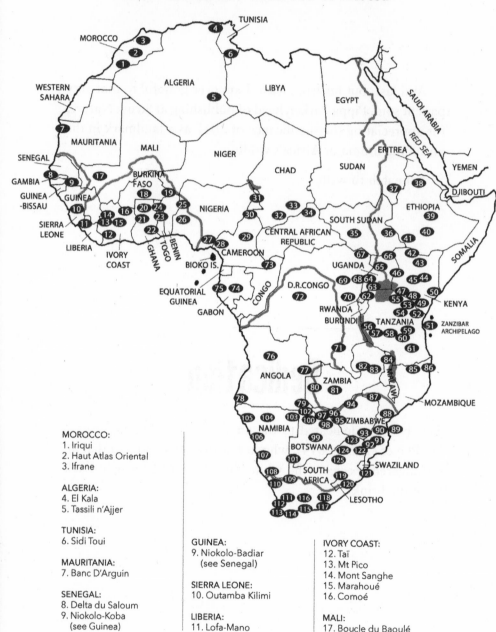

MOROCCO:
1. Iriqui
2. Haut Atlas Oriental
3. Ifrane

ALGERIA:
4. El Kala
5. Tassili n'Ajjer

TUNISIA:
6. Sidi Toui

MAURITANIA:
7. Banc D'Arguin

SENEGAL:
8. Delta du Saloum
9. Niokolo-Koba
(see Guinea)

GUINEA:
9. Niokolo-Badiar
(see Senegal)

SIERRA LEONE:
10. Outamba Kilimi

LIBERIA:
11. Lofa-Mano

IVORY COAST:
12. Taï
13. Mt Pico
14. Mont Sanghe
15. Marahoué
16. Comoé

MALI:
17. Boucle du Baoulé

BURKINA FASO:
18. Kaboré Tambi
19. W Transborder

GHANA:
20. Mole
21. Bui
22. Digya

TOGO:
23. Fazao-Malfakassa
24. Oti-Kéran

BENIN:
19. W Transborder

NIGERIA:
25. Kainji
26. Old Oyo
27. Cross River

CAMEROON:
28. Korup
29. Mbam et Djerem
30. Bénoué
31. Waza

CHAD:
32. Manda
33. Zakouma

CENTRAL AFRICAN REPUBLIC:
34. Manovo-Gounda St. Floris
73. Dzanga-Ndoki

SOUTH SUDAN:
35. Southern
36. Boma

SUDAN:
37. Dinder

ETHIOPIA:
38. Simien Mountains
39. Awash
40. Bale Mountains
41. Omo

KENYA:
42. Sibiloi
43. Marsabit
44. Meru
45. Mt. Kenya & Aberdare
46. Mount Elgon (with Uganda)
47. Maasai Mara
48. Amboseli
49. Tsavo East & Tsavo West
50. Boni

TANZANIA:
51. Jozani Chwaka Bay (Unguja Island)
52. Mkomazi
53. Arusha & Mount Kilimanjaro
54. Lake Manyara & Tarangire
55. Serenget & Ngorongoro CA
56. Mahale Mountains
57. Katavi
58. Ruaha
59. Mikumi
60. Udzungwa Mountains
61. Selous

RWANDA:
62. Akagera

UGANDA:
63. Lake Mburo
64. Queen Elizabeth (+ Rwenzori + Kibale Forest)
65. Murchison Falls
66. Kidepo valley
46. Mount Elgon (with Kenya)

DR CONGO:
67. Garamba
68. Virunga
69. Maiko
70. Kahuzi-Biéga
71. Upemba
72. Salonga

CONGO:
73. Nouabalé-Ndoki

GABON:
74. Lopé
75. Wonga-Wongue

ANGOLA:
76. Cangandala
77. Cameia
78. Iona
79. Luiana & Longa-Mavinga

ZAMBIA:
80. Liuwa Plains
81. Kafue
82. Kasanka/Bangweulu/Lavushi-Manda
83. South & North Luangwa

MALAWI:
84. Nyika

MOZAMBIQUE:
85. Niassa
86. Quirimbas
87. Magoe
88. Gorongoza
89. Bazaruto
90. Zinave
91. Banhine
92. Limpopo

ZIMBABWE:
93. Gonarezhou
94. Mana Pools
95. Hwange
96. Zambezi

BOTSWANA:
97. Chobe
98. Nxai Pan & Makgadikgadi
99. Central Kalahari
100. Moremi
101. Kgalagadi

NAMIBIA:
102. Caprivi Complex
103. Khaudom
104. Etosha
105. Skeleton Coast
106. Dorob
107. Namib-Naukluft
108. |Ai-|Ais/Richtersveld

SOUTH AFRICA:
101. Kgalagadi
108. |Ai-|Ais/Richtersveld
109. Augrabies Falls
110. West Coast
111. Tankwa Karoo
112. West Coast
113. Table Mountain
114. Agulhas
115. Garden Route
116. Karoo
117. Addo Elephant
118. Mountain Zebra
119. Golden Gate
120. Ukhahlamba Drakensberg
121. iSimangaliso
122. Kruger
123. Mapungubwe
124. Marakele
125. Pilanesberg

Map and Key courtesy of
Chris and Mathilde Stuart

1 In the beginning

We live in a zoologically impoverished world,
from which all the hugest, and fiercest,
and strangest forms have recently disappeared.

Alfred Russel Wallace, British naturalist, 1876

The word "overkill" dates from 1958 – a nasty year, in the heart of the Cold War. The world was still reeling from the aftermath of World War II, and its leaders were contemplating a still more horrific threat – nuclear war. In those days "overkill" meant to neutralise an enemy with a nuclear force more than sufficient to ensure its defeat.

"Overkill" – as a noun or a verb – can also describe anything that is over the top or done to excess. It can quite well describe, say, the compulsion that drives many people to take far more than they need whenever they have the opportunity. It's a bit like the way I behave at a hotel buffet breakfast, or the way international fishing fleets behave as they plunder the world's largest fish resources.

But make no mistake: overkill is a perfectly natural behavioural trait found in all of us predators. That's the problem.

The overkill syndrome

A classic example of an overkill was recorded by British naturalist, Maurice Burton. He described in *Nature* (1966) coming across hundreds of dead gannets on a clifftop in Scotland. He surmised from the spoor that only one fox was involved. That year, because of overpopulation, many gannets were forced to nest in the grass on top of the cliff rather than on the cliff face, where they would have been safe from predators. It had been a moonless night; but because the birds were white, the fox could easily see them. Each time it killed one, and saw another next to it, its killer instinct remained "on". The gannets would not have moved. They probably could not see the fox; in any event, they could not risk taking off in the dark, because they would have been unable to find their nests and eggs again. As long as there remained gannets within reach, the fox kept killing them.

This instinct for unbridled slaughter has been called the "henhouse syndrome", because a fox, finding its way into a chicken coop, will likewise kill every bird. The Dutch behaviourist Hans Kruuk, when he was a research zoologist at Oxford, witnessed similar scenes: "While I was studying bird behaviour in a gull colony in the north of England, a total of 1,449 adult gulls and many more young ones were found killed by foxes, without being eaten. In the Serengeti in East Africa, I found on one occasion 82 Thomson's gazelles killed and 27 maimed by spotted hyenas, and hardly utilised by the carnivores. Almost all carnivores, once they find themselves in an enclosure with suitable domestic stock, will kill and kill. In other words, man is certainly not alone amongst carnivorous species when he kills without reaping the benefit – we are dealing with a more general phenomenon."

Kruuk collected masses of data regarding what he called "surplus killing" by predators, and has written extensively on the subject.

A few years ago, near Tshokwane in Kruger National Park before the great pan – Leeupan – dried up forever, I watched a herd of wildebeest coming down to drink. It was around 10 am – the best time to be at a waterhole. It was a peaceful scene; though the animals, normally skittish when coming down to drink, were more so than usual. The herd stopped 30 metres from the water and waited. A group of juveniles went cautiously to the water's edge and began drinking. That's when the big ones decided it must be safe and descended to drink. But as soon as they dipped their muzzles into the water a lioness, at least 10 metres away but hidden in the reeds, made three enormous bounds to hit the largest male, latching onto its neck. The herd bolted. The bull was soon brought to its knees and, after perhaps four minutes, the big cat dragged the carcass up the bank to some cubs, which now tumbled into view. I was still watching when, a little later, the herd came back to the water's edge to drink. The lioness, now joined by others, was lying relaxed, picking her teeth 100 or more metres away. She showed no interest. Her killer instinct was decidedly "off". Had that same lioness found herself in a cattle kraal, however, she would have killed or savaged all within reach.

I discussed the overkill or "henhouse" syndrome with an acquaintance who recalled how, one humid summer's night in Swaziland, he became irritated by the shrillness of a chorus of frogs around his garden pond. He took his airgun and, using a miner's helmet lamp, shot the first one he saw with its sound sac inflated. Then another sounded off. He shot that too. And for the next 15 or so minutes he continued picking them off – even those that were not vocal.

He knew he was behaving irrationally, but for some time could not stop. He told me he had been so ashamed of the episode that, until our conversation, he had never spoken of it. He said, "Had the frogs scattered after the first shot I would obviously have gone back indoors. So, what drove me?"

Another vivid example of the overkill syndrome is the kind of behaviour one can witness during South Africa's winter "Sardine Run" when millions of sardines come swarming up the KwaZulu-Natal coast and are sometimes driven inshore by rampaging sharks and dolphins. Quite ordinary people appear to go berserk, rushing into the breakers to scoop up the fish; women with shopping bags and men with beer crates. Nuns have been seen catching them in their habits. People fill their car boots, or simply dump the sardines on the beach. Afterwards, when the air grows foul from the smell of rotting fish – some having been dumped quietly in the night – many participants wonder what possessed them.

Like all predators, humans have an overkill compulsion that kicks in under specific circumstances. There are many instances where humans have killed animals – or even other humans – on a scale that, in the cold light of day, seems inexplicable.

When the first European explorers, hunters and missionaries entered Africa in the 18th and 19th centuries and were confronted with its incredible abundance of wildlife, they found themselves in such a situation. Coming as they did from a rapidly urbanising world, they viewed Africa's wildlife first in wonderment, and soon as a commodity to be exploited. There was no reverence for life. Many hunters were out to make as much as they could, as fast as they could, selling ivory, exotic trophies and skins. Some just wanted to collect trophies. Nearly all viewed what they were doing as sport. Fun. The original meaning of the word "game", in a hunting context, goes back 300 years, referring to animals that could be hunted for "sport" or "the chase".

The first overkill

The Pleistocene, the epoch that saw *Homo sapiens* evolve from southern Africa's human-like apes, *Australopithecus africanus*, lasted 2½ million years and ended less than 12,000 years ago. It may have been as recently as 70,000 years ago that the first humans crossed from Africa into the Middle East.

Around 12,000 to 14,000 years ago, humans reached Siberia and crossed into North America. They used the Alaskan Land Bridge, temporarily exposed by receding sea levels.

The 2½ million years of the Pleistocene epoch had been characterised by several ice ages. When *Homo sapiens* entered North America, Canada was still buried under the ice of what was to be the last glacial period. Where Chicago is today, the ice was a kilometre deep. By the end of the Pleistocene 11,700 years ago and the subsequent retreat of the glaciers, tens of millions of square kilometres of North America had been scraped clean by the ice. At its maximum, the ice cap had reached almost down to today's New York. It had also smothered and sterilised northwestern Europe down to the Thames valley, bulldozing the landscape, obliterating forests and hills and gouging out hollows for tens of thousands of lakes. The Pleistocene had nevertheless witnessed the worldwide evolutionary climax of the animal kingdom; it produced an enormous variety of animals, among them the copious megafauna of the Americas.

The new human arrivals in North America found, no doubt to their astonishment, that the mammoths and mastodons and the giant woolly rhinoceroses of the New World were unafraid. These former lords of their domain were not to know that the little interlopers were highly skilled and fearless plains hunters carrying the most advanced weapon of the day, the Clovis spear. These new super-predators were the descendants of the early African hunters who had learned to track and kill megafauna up to the size of six-tonne elephants. They had honed their skills as they trekked across Asia and the Siberian plains – the most difficult of hunting grounds, for there was almost no cover. Over the millennia, the animals of Asia had learned to flee from them, thus forcing the hunters to constantly refine their techniques.

The animals did not flee in North America.

The late Paul S. Martin of the University of Arizona wrote in 1967 of the "Pleistocene overkill". He described how, in a relatively short time, the immigrant hunters extinguished not just individual species but whole groups of species. Wherever humans arrived, "extinctions skyrocketed," said Martin. Around the world, 90% of the species that had emerged from the Pleistocene became extinct. Climate change may also have played a role here; but these mammals had evolved, and survived, through many climate changes. Two hundred genera disappeared in short order. *Homo sapiens* caused or accelerated the extinction of the woolly rhinoceroses, mammoths, mastodons, giant camels, native horses, and ground sloths that looked like something Dr Seuss dreamt up; cave bears and giant elk with antlers as a wide as a bus. With them disappeared heavyweight scavengers and predators such as the dire wolf and the powerful sabre-tooth cats. One can trace the extinctions as humans migrated southwards, down America. They reached Central and South America in appreciable numbers around 11,000 years ago, and that is when 80% of these regions' megafauna disappeared. Again, climate change may have played a role – the last great Ice Age was reaching its end – but the "smoking gun" is the presence of Clovis spearheads, their age established by precise carbon-14 dating, among the bones. To kill an animal with such a weapon, the hunters must have been able to approach quite close to their unsuspecting quarry.

Of North America's big avian scavengers, only the Californian condor survives. And only just.

It's difficult to appreciate just how recent and sudden this global overkill was. In the same period, less adventurous though equally resourceful humans stayed behind in Asia and in southern Europe, establishing settlements and croplands, and corralling the first aurochs – the shaggy bovines from which today's cattle are descended. Geologically speaking we are talking about yesterday.

The fascinating anomaly is that on the very continent from which humans originated and where they developed their hunting skills, there was no catastrophic megafaunal overkill. The vast African savanna, mainly down the eastern side of the continent, was, throughout the epoch, teeming with grazing, browsing and predatory animals – pachyderms, big cats and dozens of species of antelope. In many places it still is. It is the world's last surviving preserve of the Pleistocene.

But Africa's megafauna did not survive *in spite of* predatory humans. It survived *because* of them.

Africa's mammals had witnessed the evolution of humans; they had watched them graduate from stone-throwing, club-wielding, aggressive little australopithecine scavenger/hunters into more gracile, larger-brained, athletic spear throwers. As humans developed greater skills and more sophisticated weapons, so the animals learned to keep their distance. Baboons today have developed a whole range of flight distances depending on whether it's a human male approaching, or a female, or a child – and whether the male is armed or is empty-handed.

It was only in the 18th and 19th centuries, when hunters acquired guns, that the large mammals of Africa became seriously threatened.

It is well established through carbon-14 dating that, by 45,000 years ago, bands of humans had reached Southeast Asia. Sea levels were much lower at the time, and many humans island-hopped to Australia. There followed the rapid extinction of Australia's hippo-sized marsupial herbivores, carnivorous kangaroos, giant lizards, tortoises big enough to ride, and several large flightless birds.

The planet's most recent wave of extinctions did not involve hunters at all; it involved mariners. From the 15th century – the Age of Exploration – navigators such as James Cook set sail across the oceans and sought provisions from uninhabited islands. They discovered hitherto unknown, weird and wonderful creatures, and set about eating them. From one island alone, Cook carried off 300 live turtles to replenish his ship's protein stock.

Island animals, which had no natural enemies, would have been unfazed as they watched the first humans wade ashore. On some islands there were ratites, far, far larger even than today's largest example, the African ostrich. Madagascar's elephant bird – extinguished in the 17th century – weighed up to half a tonne. The ratites saw no reason to flee; indeed, they had nowhere to flee anyway.

Each one of the big island birds was eradicated, with the exception of the smallest – New Zealand's chicken-sized kiwi. According to the International Union for Conservation of Nature (IUCN), of the five existing species of kiwi, one is "critically endangered" (i.e. one category above "extinct"), another is "endangered", and two are currently "vulnerable".

Nearly all the extinctions in the world since the 15th century have been of island species. In the last 200 years, Hawaii has lost a third of its bird species – including some of astonishing beauty – not necessarily directly killed by humans but through other anthropogenic causes such as the introduction of foreign animals. Sailors, tiring of their pet monkeys, cats, goats, pigs and snakes, dumped them ashore, where they often made short work of the local wildlife. The most pernicious of our companions was the rat; it was extremely successful, both as a migrant and as an agent of the extinction of bird species.

It was probably egg-eating monkeys that tipped the fat, 20-kilogram, flightless pigeon, the dodo, into oblivion; first seen in 1505, it was extinct by 1681. The flightless goose-like Rodrigues solitaire was another overgrown flightless pigeon. It disappeared about a century after its discovery.

The Holocene and beyond

When the Pleistocene Epoch ended 11,700 years ago, it was replaced by the Holocene, or "recent", epoch, in which we now live. At the dawn of the Holocene there were no permanent structures anywhere; no roads, no towns and no nations; the air was clear except for sporadic volcanic eruptions as well as natural and anthropogenic grass and forest fires; the rivers and the seas were uncontaminated by industrial and agricultural chemicals and plastics. There were no dams and no nuclear waste; and the billions of tonnes of carbon (from coal and oil) that have now altered the nature of this planet's atmosphere were still locked harmlessly away underground.

The Indo-Pacific islands were untouched by humans.

The label "Holocene" is no longer appropriate. We have changed the planet's chemistry and its climate. Forests have become deserts. The seas – the planet's final sink – have been insanely abused. We have wrested the process of evolution from nature, deciding which animals will live – and where.

We need to define a new epoch. How about the "Anthropocene" – the human epoch? The word was coined by Paul Crutzen, a Dutch chemist and Nobel Laureate, and popularised by Elizabeth Colbert in her 2014 bestseller, *The Sixth Extinction*. In August 2016, scientists attending the International Geological Congress in Cape Town urged that we accept that the Holocene has ended and the Anthropocene epoch – the age of man – is well advanced. What on earth will it bring?

2 The rifle brigade

"'Unting is all that's worth living for – all time
is lost wot is not spent in 'unting – it's the sport
of kings, the image of war without its guilt, and
only five-and-twenty percent of its danger.'"

Robert Smith Surtees, *Jorrocks' Jaunts and Jollities* (London, 1838)

The antics of one particular Englishman, Sir William
Cornwallis Harris (1807–1848), epitomised the commonly
held European and American attitude regarding "sport
hunting" in Africa. This attitude began with the introduction
of the firearm and prevailed deep into the 20th century. Harris
was a soldier, fine artist, terrible writer, excruciating poet and
pathological egotist. In 1836 he was sent to South Africa on
sick leave by the British army in India. He set off northwards
from the Cape to the virtually unknown and unmapped region
north of the River Vaal. His ox-wagons carried two tonnes of
lead for making bullets en route.

Harris wrote one of the best-known volumes of Africana,
Wild Sports of Southern Africa (1840), in which he tells us:
"Hunting, from the earliest antiquity, has formed no less the
favourite pastime of the mightiest monarchs, than the chosen
exercise of the most exalted heroes. Poets and minstrels have
made the *merrye greene woode* the theme and burden of their
wild song. Philosophers and sages have lauded the sylvan
craft, as combining exercise to the body, with delight and
entertainment to the mind; whilst painters and sculptors have
made it the subject of the noblest creations of their skill and

10

genius." Describing hunting as "this noble diversion", which he sees as "part of civilisation", he boasts how he had shot a hippopotamus and had "torn the much-prized ivory from his giant jaws ... plucked the horn from the saucy nose of the Rhinoceros. I have stripped the proud spolia from the shaggy shoulder of the 'king of beasts'." Harris was typical of the Britons of his time – indeed of most Europeans and Americans too – in the quite shameless and soulless way he viewed wild animals. He describes, with undisguised pride, how, in the Karoo – South Africa's semi-desert – he slaughtered, willy-nilly, anything he saw. One day, following up a herd of "brindled gnoos" (blue wildebeest), he watched them joined by more wildebeest, zebra, tsessebe and hartebeest. They were "pouring down from every quarter ... until the landscape absolutely presented a moving mass of game. Closing with the front ranks and riding parallel to the cohort in order to escape the dust and pebbles which were cast up by their hooves, I dismounted – firing both barrels of my rifle into the retreating phalanx and leaving the ground behind me strewn with the slain ... still unsatisfied, I could not resist the temptation of mixing yet again with the fugitives, firing and reloading ..."

He describes riding down two eland, chasing them "until their grey sides became white with froth, foam fell in strings from their mouths, grease from their nostrils" – they were "steaming" he said, and finally, exhausted, they stopped and looked at him "imploringly". Our hero shot them both.

Eland became his favourite meat, and he boasts of never having missed the opportunity of "levying a tax upon their herds". Finding hartebeest meat unpalatable, he shot them purely for fun. On seeing a herd of 400 elephants in the Cashan Mountains (now the Magaliesberg), he fired into the herd as it passed to see how many he could hit.

Harris refers to humans as "the lords of creation" and wildlife as "the foe"; on one occasion, having fired some balls into a rhino, he "felt compelled to abstain from further hostilities".

He writes of the extraordinary number of white rhino he found in the Limpopo valley and how, as soon as the draft oxen were unyoked, "the whole party in the regular routine of business, having assumed their weapons, proceeded to dislodge the enemy ... every individual came in for a share of cold lead."

Talk of "war without its guilt ..."

Harris writes of "humbling" wild animals. Such language is most revealing.

Less than a decade later the tall, eccentric, kilted Scotsman, Roualeyn Gordon-Cumming, entered the scene and carved his way from the Eastern Cape to Central Africa, shooting almost anything he saw. On one occasion he shot a horse, and on another two oxen. He thought they were game.

One night he crept up on an elephant in the dark, and could just make out its bulk several metres way. He blindly shot into the shape, not knowing where he might have hit it; he hoped to have wounded it sufficiently for it not to move far. Next day, climbing a hillock, "to my inexpressible gratification beheld a group of nine or ten quietly browsing". They were all female. At this point, Gordon-Cumming adopts the third person and writes how "he feasts his eyes upon the enchanting sight ... a council of war is hastily held". Then, "burning with impatience to commence the attack", he nevertheless "resolved to enjoy the pleasure of watching their movements for a little" before firing. He shot one cow which he believed was mortally wounded and saw a second cow come to her assistance. He gave this one "both barrels (and) foolishly allowed her to escape while I amused myself with the first". Later, he saw two cows, each with a calf. He shot both, but makes no further mention of the calves; nor does he mention whether the elephant he shot the night before was still around.

Only once does Gordon-Cumming appear to reflect on what he is doing, remarking that he was "making happy the starving families of hundreds of Bechuanas and Bakalahari tribes that followed the hunt".

Indeed, lots of animals slaughtered during 19th-century expeditions were used to feed staff. Some long-ranging safaris were followed by as many as 2,000 people attracted by the constant supply of surplus meat and skins.

Daily, Gordon-Cumming shot all he could see, including black rhino and white, the latter being very common. He shot one rhino purely for lion bait – lion being his favourite prey. Like Cornwallis Harris, he often calls his quarry "noble", and even refers to "noble tusks".

He rode down a magnificent bull giraffe just to collect its noble tail.

Gordon-Cumming's 1860 book, *The Lion Hunter, in the Days when all of South Africa was Virgin Hunting Field,* becomes repetitive and boring – a kind of hunting pornography; a long catalogue of slaughter. Towards its end he records, "I had now shot noble specimens of every sort of game in South Africa except a few smaller bucks common in the colony – and the hippo".

He soon added hippo to his list. He shot several, all with his usual abandon – even females with calves. He did all of this with a rifle that required loading with powder and a ball of lead using a ramrod. Imagine the carnage he would have wrought with a modern repeater rifle. Some pachyderms absorbed 30 and more bullets, and many hunters found their trophies already had ancient bullets embedded in them.

In many 19th-century accounts, hunters seemed to imagine they were on a military mission.

When Prince Alfred, Prince of Wales, the 16-year-old second son of Queen Victoria, visited South Africa in 1860, a hunt was organised in his honour. This was on the farm Bainsvlei on the road between Bloemfontein and Kimberley. Days before his visit, the local Sothos were employed to encircle a great plain and drive its wild animals towards the farmstead.

It was, says John Pringle in *The Conservationists and the Killers (1982)*, the greatest slaughter in history. He quotes a witness, Major General J. J. Bisset:

"Early in the morning of 24th August 1860 His Royal Highness and the shooting party of 25 guns in all started from Mr Bain's farm ... followed by a considerable number of ladies and gentlemen.

"Towards 2pm clouds of dust rising from all quarters, and the blank gunshots of the farm hands told that the game had been cheated out of their afternoon siesta and were fairly on foot ... Then the Prince took to horse as did all (ladies included) ...

"And the battle commenced by the prince bringing down a great wildebeest or gnu. This ferocious-looking beast turned on his Royal Highness on being wounded and received a second ball which rolled him over. This was the sign for the general onslaught.

"The hunting party advanced up the plain in extended order and masses of game kept breaking through as the pressure of the coming streams of antelope, quaggas, zebras, blesbok, elands, ostriches, hartebeests, wildebeests, koedoes, etc., etc., came pouring on towards us and checked by our fire commenced to whirl. The plain in which we were was of vast extent – and the whole of the extent was one moving mass of game. The gaps between the mountains on all sides of this plain were stopped by a living line of men, and we were in the midst of this whirling throng firing at great game at not 25 yards distance as fast as we could load. The Prince fired as fast as guns could be handed to him, for Currie rode on one side and I rode on the other, and we alternately handed guns to him as he discharged his own. As the circle narrowed there really was considerable danger from the game breaking through for when a stampede took place so much dust arose that you were in danger of being trampled to death. It became very exciting to see great beasts, larger than horses, rolling over from right to left shot not ten paces from you, and also charging down with their great horns lowered as if they were coming right at you ...

"During the great slaughter of the day the circle of natives was closing in and the mass of game became so pressed together at last that the Prince and Currie took to their hunting hog spears and charged into the midst, driving home the 'Paget blades' into the infuriated animals.

"The slaughter was tremendous considering that it did not endure beyond an hour. How many fell on the spot or died afterwards of their wounds, or were caught by the farm hands would be difficult to tell. The Prince shot 24.

"The fact was that the Prince and suite were weary of the slaughter ... and most of the sportsmen looked more like butchers than sportsmen from being so covered in blood. His Royal Highness and Currie were red up to their shoulders from using the spear."

It was indeed a shameful episode; yet the women, according to the major-general, clapped and shouted excitedly from the farm stoep. None of them realised they had just witnessed the last formal quagga hunt. Would they have cared, I wonder? The last quagga *(Equus quagga)* died in Amsterdam Zoo 23 years later; only when the zoo requested a replacement was it realised that the species no longer existed.

Mass slaughter was sometimes practised by the Zulu in the 19th century. They would hold game drives and chase animals into areas where they had prepared deep pits and barriers. The hunts were part of their military training, and large numbers of young warriors, carrying shields and assegais (spears), would stampede the animals. But such hunts were carefully scheduled to allow populations to recover. In between, no hunting was allowed in the area. Poaching was punishable by being clubbed to death – the most effective game law, I suppose, in the history of conservation.

The 19th century stands out as perhaps the most heartless in history when it comes to our relationship with our animal contemporaries. Things did not improve much until well into the 20th century. The concept of "animal rights" would have been laughed at 150 years ago. In those days, even human rights were unthinkable in most countries. In Africa, both the colonists and the Africans themselves were using and abusing slaves, a practice that continued well into the 20th century.

Extinctions are often abrupt affairs. Consider the fate of America's passenger pigeon. There were hundreds of millions – even, as some suggest, billions – of these pigeons. They might have been the most numerous bird on Earth in the 19th century. Their flocks bred in the vast virgin forests that, at the time, covered most of the United States. Passing flocks frequently blotted out the sun – for hours according to some accounts. In 1890 the flocks darkened the sky over New York City and Philadelphia, and people standing on rooftops shot into them, just for the hell of it. New York restaurateurs brought in wagon-loads of them. By mid-century, the flocks were thinning out in parts, and the state of Ohio suggested that the harvesting of the pigeons needed to be controlled; but a committee decided the bird needed no protection.

In 1871 a Wisconsin nesting was estimated to be "seventy-five miles long and 10–15 miles across", according to Peter Matthiessen in his classic, *Wildlife in America* (1959). It was estimated that this single nesting was shared by "136 million birds". Whatever the true figure, it was enough to attract "hunters" from far and wide, armed with nets, guns and fire. In a few days the area was laid waste, and millions of dead birds were shipped to the cities at a few cents a dozen.

Concurrently with this kind of slaughter, the large-scale harvesting of timber for housing and for railway sleepers resulted in the rapid destruction of the passenger pigeons' woodland habitat. This no doubt played a major role in the eventual extermination of the pigeons. In 1899 the last wild passenger pigeon known to have been shot fell from the sky in Wisconsin. Fifteen years later, on 1 September 1914, Martha, the last surviving pigeon, died in a cage in Cincinnati Zoo after years in captivity. Many witnessed her death, for she had been showing signs of distress during the morning; and all who stood there knew she was the last of her kind on Earth.

Equally sad was the wanton destruction of the North American bison. The bison (buffalo), whose massive herds darkened the plains, stood two metres tall and weighed close to a tonne. It was the largest survivor of America's Pleistocene plains mammals. It was relied upon by native Indians for meat, clothing, bedding, teepee walls and saddlecloths, and its sinews provided cordage and bowstrings. Not that the Indians were, towards the end, any more respectful of the bison than were the settlers. The tribes, now armed with guns, would sometimes leave the meadows strewn with carcasses, having removed just the tongues, which they relished. The buffalo were helpless in the face of mounted hunters equipped with rifles. The completion of the Pacific Railway in 1869 helped seal their fate. Matthiessen says that between 1872 and 1874, well over a million bison were shot annually in the southern ranges.

William F. "Buffalo Bill" Cody claimed to have shot 4,280 buffalo in 18 months to provide meat for railway workers. His description of a mounted hunt demonstrates what a "turkey shoot" it was.

"I have killed from 25 to 40 buffalo while the herd was circling (in confusion), and they would all be dropped very close together, that is to say, in a space covering five acres ..."

By the dawn of the 20th century, only two remnant herds were left. Yellowstone Park sheltered "twenty-odd" and Lost Park in Colorado (not far from Denver) provided room for the others. The latter were eventually picked off by hunters/ taxidermists before protective legislation could be introduced. By the beginning of the 20th century, the numbers had reached several hundred. Today there are at least 500,000.

The 19th- and 20th-century overkill all but wiped out another large herbivore, the saiga antelope of Eurasia. The saiga, which once roamed from Britain to Siberia, at a time when the English Channel did not exist, numbered hundreds upon hundreds of millions. Their enormous herds moved over the steppe like cloud shadows.

They were nearly extinct by the 1920s – driven to the brink by habitat destruction and hunting. They had recovered to a certain extent by the 1950s, when they apparently numbered around 2 million – nearly all on the Russian Steppe. But the collapse of the Soviet Union in 1989 led to their uncontrolled slaughter. This was mostly because the Chinese, who had long since wiped out their own herds, valued their horns as medicine and as an aphrodisiac. The saiga's population is said to be as low as 50,000 and the species is categorised as "CR" ("critically endangered") in the IUCN's Red List of Threatened Species. This is just one better than the next category, which is "E".

E is for Extinct.

3 The predator's way

Man's nature is not essentially evil.
Brute nature has been known to yield
to the influence of love. You must never
despair of human nature.

Mahatma Gandhi

In 2016 the journal *Nature* recorded a chilling find at Nataruk near Kenya's Lake Turkana. Twenty-seven skeletons were found of men, women and children; some had apparently been bound hand and foot before being clubbed to death. Carbon dating shows the massacre took place at the start of the Holocene, 10,000 years ago.

Until this discovery, it had been assumed that humans emerged from the Pleistocene leading innocent lives, hunting and gathering in a world whose human population was relatively sparse and scattered. The Turkana discovery led some anthropologists to suggest that warfare pre-dated agriculture – that we were at each other's throats long before we settled down in permanent villages and grew crops. The earliest evidence of concerted social strife, up to then, was a "war grave" excavated at Darmstadt, Germany, dated as 7,000 years old. Mass aggression, anthropologists had assumed, came after the agricultural revolution when tribes and bands of humans began to assume ownership of land, thus causing jealousy among neighbouring communities.

Describing the Nataruk episode, Robert Foley of Cambridge's Leverhulme Centre for Human Evolutionary

19

Studies suggested that violence seems to have been as much part of human nature as altruism. The Nataruk event rekindled the debate about the character of humankind. What has driven us? What sort of creatures are we?

The questions have haunted behaviourists for centuries and continue to do so.

Maybe it was our lack of fangs, claws, horns and fleetness of foot? Dawn Man, because of his unique vulnerability as a two-legged animal, must have felt uncomfortably inferior when walking in the bush – indeed, I still feel terribly respectful when walking, unarmed, in the wilds with lions, elephants and buffalo around. Yet, here we evolved, weighing in at 40–80 kilograms, living among creatures that were faster and stronger and possessed fangs like marlinspikes. Throwing stones wasn't enough. So we developed the spear; and for 2 million years – in fact for 99% of our history – we relied on it for defence and, particularly, attack. We were now one up on all other creatures: we could kill at a distance.

That is where overkill began. We were now able to settle disputes between ourselves by killing at a distance. No longer did we have to fight body to body like the other animals who, characteristically, rarely killed others of their own species, being satisfied with witnessing the submission of their opponents. Even a human such as an infantryman, when fighting at close quarters and having incapacitated an enemy, will rarely then finish him off. A normal reaction is to feel compassion for somebody lying, defeated, at one's feet. Yet train even an average family man as a bomber pilot and he will, without any overriding feeling of guilt, bomb a city and tear apart and incinerate men, women and children by the hundreds.

The spear, and ultimately the gun, allowed us to "have dominion ... over all the Earth" as the King James version of the Bible unfortunately exhorted us.

Robert Ardrey and Raymond Dart

The universal debate regarding our unique propensity to go to war and kill on a scale that could be our own undoing went up a notch in the 1960s when the science writer, Broadway playwright and journalist Robert Ardrey proposed in *African Genesis* that we were "born killers". His 1961 bestseller began with this eloquent passage:

"Not in innocence, and not in Asia, was mankind born. The home of our fathers was that African highland reaching north from the Cape to the lakes of the Nile. Here we came about – slowly, ever so slowly – on a sky-swept savanna glowing with menace ... Children of all animal kind, we inherited many a social nicety as well as the predator's way. But the most significant of all our gifts, as things turned out, was the legacy bequeathed us by the killer apes, our immediate forebears. Even in the first long days of our beginnings we held in our hand the weapon, an instrument somewhat older than ourselves."

Although Ardrey's book is in some respects outdated, it still gives a fascinating and brilliantly written insight into the early years of hominid research in Africa. The science of palaeo-anthropology – the study of the origins and way of life of our ancestors – was riven with intense and often quite boisterous debate in mid-century.

In 1961, during an 18-month stay in New Zealand, I was asked to serialise Ardrey's book. I knew many of the characters he described and had been on expeditions with them. As I read, my mind kept going back to a mountain range about 40 minutes by car north of where I lived in Johannesburg – the Magaliesberg. To get to it one drives through beautiful bush-covered hills honeycombed with caves, many of which are rich in fossils. The range itself, from the air, appears to be a 120-kilometre-long ocean roller sweeping towards the south, where it falls away in an escarpment whitewashed in places by Cape vulture droppings (this is one of the vulture's very few breeding areas).

The range is 2.5 billion years old – one of the oldest mountain ranges on Earth. It was protected from erosion for hundreds of millions of years by being buried beneath another geological system, which has since eroded away. I used to climb to its crest at dawn most Sundays, find a comfortable rock and sit and study the crumpled, thickly wooded hills to the south and the toothy outline of Johannesburg 40 kilometres away on the horizon.

Until about 1840, the mountains and the bush-covered hills supported a superabundance of wildlife. By 1900 the region had largely been hunted out – gone were the great herds of elephant that Cornwallis Harris had fired into. Gone, too, were the once-abundant white rhinoceroses, the giraffe, the buffalo and a dozen species of antelope. This included that most magnificent of buck, the sable antelope with its great curved horns, first described in these mountains by Cornwallis Harris; it was known as "Harris' buck" for years. There are still some wild antelope, and the leopard and brown hyena still hunt the mountain's secret places.

To my right, in the middle distance, Pelindaba's nuclear research station jutted out from the Daspoort range. Further right I could see a ridge where there are more fossiliferous caves – some have walls white with fossils. Those caves were to leap into the headlines in the 1940s and again at the dawn of the 21st century when a young American, Lee Berger, a Kansas PhD, came on to the stage and turned humankind's lineage on its head. Berger recognised the Magaliesberg and its parallel ridges as one of the world's greatest repositories of palaeontological secrets.

Since 1999, there have been signboards in the valley declaring the region "The Cradle of Humankind". There's a sign with the same wording at Tanzania's Olduvai Gorge – famous for its collection of early *Homo* skulls. The rivalry between the two sites and their teams of scientists has been long and fascinating, often noisy – and I was privileged, at its peak, to have had a ringside seat.

Until 2013 only the fossilised bones of "apemen" *(Australopithecus africanus)* had been found in the mountains. More were found further north at Makapansgat in the Limpopo valley. This led the East African palaeontologists to declare – sometimes rather derisively – that South Africa's australopithecines were a dead end in hominid evolution. Humanity, they said, evolved from the australopithecines found 4,000 kilometres north in East Africa.

Ardrey came to South Africa in 1955 to write a series of articles on the country. While here, he received a message from a friend at Yale saying "a South African scientist is about to explode a philosophical bomb, a positive demonstration that the first recognisably human assertion was the capacity for murder". The scientist was Raymond Dart, an immigrant anatomist from Queensland, Australia. In March that year the two men met, and their years of dialogue began.

At the time, there was good reason to debate humanity's beginnings and whether our "killer instinct" would be our undoing. The turmoil in power politics and the vitriol in international relations in the 1960s were such that Willy Brandt, Chancellor of West Germany, voiced his conviction that humankind would not survive the 20th century. World War II was still fresh in many minds, and Russia's and America's political and military leaders were full of adrenaline. Just to make a point, in 1962 Russia detonated, underground, a nuclear bomb with a kilotonnage that is yet to be surpassed.

The deadliness of the situation was brought home to me in 2015 when two fellow members of Johannesburg's RAF Officers' Club, Louis Nel and Colin Francis, described what it was like in 1962 when they were in Britain's Royal Air Force

Bomber Command. Louis described how, as a 26-year-old flight lieutenant, he routinely had to take off in a Vulcan B2 bomber loaded with a nuclear bomb. The crew's target was Moscow's vast state-owned department store GUM, because this massive landmark was central enough to ensure the obliteration of the Russian capital should the USSR make a false move. This was the time of the Cuban missile crisis, when the world tottered on the very brink of World War III. The Russian Navy was sailing to Cuba to arm a nuclear missile base just 60 kilometres off America's Florida coast. The American President, J. F. Kennedy, issued an ultimatum; and finally, the Russians turned the fleet around, on the promise that the Americans would dismantle their own nuclear missile bases in Turkey, on the border of the Soviet Union.

From this type of brinkmanship did the acronym MAD (Mutually Assured Destruction) join "overkill" in the English language.

Homo sapiens, "man the wise", tends to regard the dinosaurs as losers, though they endured for 135 million years. Yet here we were on the verge of self-inflicted oblivion after a mere 200,000.

That was why many people, like Dart, asserted that we were saddled with the legacy of the "killer apes". Dart was to die in 1988, aged 96, without ever changing his mind on that score.

The Taung Child and Piltdown Man

In 1923, at the age of 32, Raymond Dart became head of anatomy at Johannesburg's new University of the Witwatersrand. He'd been in South Africa less than a year and badly needed students and funds. He was slowly accumulating anatomical specimens for the school's empty shelves when a student, Josephine Salmon, told him that a friend's father had a fossilised baboon skull on his mantelpiece. It had been unearthed during blasting in a lime quarry at Taung in the semi-arid Northern Cape, 400 kilometres west of Johannesburg. Dart was intrigued because, at that stage, no fossilised primate skull had been found in South Africa.

When he saw the face peering out from its rocky matrix, Dart immediately realised that this was no baboon's skull. He was staring into the smooth facial bones of a small, remarkably human-looking child. What he could see of the cranium revealed it had a far larger brain than a baboon or even a chimp. Equally interesting were its teeth; unlike apes and monkeys, it had no fangs. Most important of all, the opening at the base of the child's skull, where the spine would have connected, was well forward, indicating that the creature had mostly stood upright. Dart named it, cautiously, *Australopithecus africanus*, the "southern ape of Africa".

Dart described the "Taung Child" as a member of "an extinct race of apes intermediate between living anthropoids and man". This was about a century after Charles Darwin had predicted that, one day, a fossil primate would be found that was neither ape nor human, but somewhere in between. Darwin had even suggested it was likely to be found in Africa.

The world's leading science journal, *Nature*, showed a mysterious reluctance to publish Dart's find. Meanwhile the Johannesburg newspaper *The Star*, out of courtesy, sat on the story for weeks, having agreed to wait for *Nature* to publish. In January 1925, *The Star*'s editor, Charles Don, who was interested in palaeontology, told *Nature* he was going ahead regardless; and on 3 February the newspaper published the story under the headline "The Missing Link?". *Nature* published four days later; the reason for the journal's reluctance soon became evident.

It transpired that *Nature* was being pressured by a lobby of top British anthropologists that had staked its reputation on the 1912 discovery of a skull at Piltdown in Sussex. Britain's "Piltdown Man" had an ape-like lower jaw and a brain as big as that of a modern human. It apparently made sense – at least to the British Museum – that the missing link should turn out to be a big-brained Englishman.

Sir Arthur Smith Woodward, one of Piltdown Man's discoverers, was particularly venomous in his criticism of Dart's discovery, saying that the Taung skull was that of a modern chimpanzee. Sir Arthur Keith stated in a letter to *Nature* that Dart's claim was "preposterous". He wrote that "the skull is that of a young anthropoid ape ... showing so many points of affinity with the two living African anthropoids, the gorilla and chimpanzee, that there cannot be a moment's hesitation in placing the fossil form in this living group". Dart, meanwhile, could see that there was something fishy about the Piltdown discovery. However, there the matter was to rest for many years.

In South Africa, to strengthen Dart's hypothesis, the search was now on for an adult australopithecine.

In 1936, the 70-year-old Robert Broom came out of retirement as a medical practitioner and took up the challenge. He was a Scot, short in stature, short in patience and formal in dress. Broom, who often wore a butterfly collar, jacket, tie and waistcoat when working at a site, was already an internationally respected palaeontologist and had discovered many fossilised examples of what he called "warm-blooded reptiles" – the missing links, if you like, between the early reptiles and the rise of the mammals.

In 1947 Broom was excavating an old lime quarry at the Sterkfontein Caves in the foothills of the Magaliesberg where local children were selling fossils for a few pennies. He had by now become impatient and, much to the alarm of his colleagues, had resorted to using dynamite and pickaxes. Dynamite, to a palaeontologist, is what a hacksaw is to a heart surgeon. To his joy, out rolled an adult australopithecine skull. Okay, it was not quite like that – the skull was in two pieces – but it was clearly an adult apeman skull, the most perfect australopithecine relic thus far.

The new skull left the northern scientists stubbornly unimpressed. Broom lived another four years, alas, not long enough to witness the northerners' humiliation. When advanced dating techniques entered the picture it was revealed, in 1953, that Piltdown Man was an astonishingly crude hoax. The perpetrator, whoever he was, had used the stained lower jaw of a modern orangutan whose teeth had been filed down to disguise the fact that this was an ape's jaw. The cranium was that of a modern human.

Only now did the humbled British anthropologists turn their attention to Africa. But it was East Africa that ultimately benefited from their attention because, by then, the international science community was boycotting South Africa on account of its apartheid policy. The country was to remain in the shadows for four decades. The Calvinist conservatives who held power at that time were creationists who argued that blacks and whites were "created" separately and even, some declared, had separate heavens. This government had no interest in funding palaeo-anthropology; evolution was not allowed to be discussed in government schools and many church schools also barred the subject.

Apartheid came to an abrupt end in 1990. The new South African government, elected in 1994, was keen to fund research into human origins. For years, the evidence had been pointing to the likelihood that humanity originated in Africa. But East Africa continued to attract most of the research, because although the Magaliesberg region had yielded many "apeman" bones as well as the world's earliest known stone tools, it would be another 23 years before Lee Berger discovered, in a cave 30 metres underground, the bones of 15 early humanoid individuals – eight children, five adults and two adolescents – a whole heap of holy grail. They were members of a previously unknown but possibly indirect ancestor of *Homo sapiens*: *H. naledi*.

The co-operative hypothesis

On one memorable weekend in the summer of 1964, I sat around a campfire in the mountains with Dart, Phillip Tobias, James Kitching, and a dozen others, under a night sky so clear and moonless that it was white with stars. Dart was in his element. The professor reversed his old Rover up to where we sat and removed a Bakers' Biscuits tin from the boot. From it, he withdrew a bundle of cotton wool and, from that, in slow motion, he dramatically withdrew science's most famous skull – known as the Taung Child. Until then, this fossilised skull of a creature that was "neither ape nor man but somewhere in between" had never been displayed outside Wits Medical School.

Dart was interested in amateur theatre and he often resorted to dramatics when lecturing. In the firelight, hunching his shoulders up around his ears and wielding a donkey's axe-like scapula above his head, he was transformed into an australopithecine. One quite forgot the collar, tie and tweed jacket he was wearing (seriously) as he mimicked the fierce little apeman's action when killing baboons – or, perhaps, when killing fellow apemen. As Dart transported us back a couple of million years, we watched spellbound, while a satellite – the first some of us had ever seen – crawled across the sky behind him.

The fireside debate touched on human behaviour and while I forget the details, something was said that made me dwell, in my weekly science column, on our innate behavioural patterns; and I suggested that clubs and spears would not have been enough to ensure our success as a species. To have survived and thrived in Africa, apart from the ability to run like hell, hominids must have had a more constructive, a more overriding instinct.

Naively, I suggested our strongest urge was to love and be loved. The theory that we were pathologically driven by "the legacy bequeathed us by the killer apes", as Ardrey put it, was hard to accept. I argued that for the vast majority of our ancestors, no aggression or weapons of assault would have been needed to pick berries or knap stones for tools and weapons, to skin animals or chase after kids. They would have had no reason to kill. And even for the small number who hunted, there was no aggression in hunting either. Some people today may be hunters because (as hunters argue) of some atavistic instinct, but they are not driven by aggression, any more than a lion is when hunting impala. A fox doesn't hate chickens or have anything against rabbits.

Among existing hunter-gatherer communities today, such as the San ("Bushmen") in southern Africa, the "gathering" function, and not the hunting function, is the mainstay of survival. Only a tiny minority – maybe one or two in a thousand, would have had to kill anything that could be described as megafauna. For every hunter, hundreds would have been needed to do nothing more adventurous than shaping stone axes, cleavers, scrapers and spearheads, butchering carcasses, collecting fuel and keeping the hearth fire from going out.

Early man had available a whole smörgåsbord of easily procured bush food – protein-rich insects and their larvae, birds' eggs, nestlings, small mammals and reptiles caught in snares. That's how the only other terrestrial primates, the baboons and gorillas, feed themselves.

Meat was a bonanza for humans, as it still is among most of the world's people. It was a quick fix for protein and allowed humans some respite from having to forage for hours on end; instead, they were able to spend more time interacting with the family and the tribe. But if it was not our prowess as killers, then what was it that enabled Dawn Man, who was considerably smaller than today's humans, to survive and thrive in Africa – of all places?

Richard Leakey, the Kenyan fossil-hunter and head of Kenya Wildlife Service, suggested in his 1977 book, *Origin*, that the basis of our success was "co-operation". We humans survived because we learned to act as a team. Fangless and clawless though we were, we could stand together and defend ourselves on Ardrey's grassland "glowing with menace".

What, then, of war? Where did that come from? The ability to wage war is, ironically, a demonstration of a very high order of Leakey's co-operative imperative. But to fight en masse to the death we have first to be primed by political exhortations, be worked up by propaganda and hear lots of drums. The "killer mode" is not easily switched on. Adam Zamoyski, who analyses Napoleon's retreat from Moscow in his 2005 book, *1812*, mentions how soldiers of the *Grande Armée* could be roused to acts of selfless courage by a mixture of patriotism, esprit de corps and love of their Emperor (Napoleon) – but they did not indulge in butchery. To kill, the soldiers needed constant hyping up by their commanders. Zamoyski mentions a Lieutenant Blaze de Barry who talked of "soldiers fighting without hating each other". De Barry, who had fought in many campaigns, said, "During a ceasefire, we would often visit the enemy's encampment and while we were ready to murder each other at the first signal, we were nonetheless prepared to help each other if the occasion presented itself."

A common sight after a pitched battle in most wars is the soldiers' compassion for the wounded, enemy or not. Once an enemy is wounded, the reptilian brain ceases to flood the system with anxiety hormones; and so the killer compulsion switches off.

After the Battle of Agincourt, England's King Henry V ordered the slaughter of the French prisoners. The defeated French prisoners greatly outnumbered Henry's victorious army, and he feared they might snatch up the discarded weapons strewn about the field and set upon the victors. Importantly, Henry was far from the battlefield; his men were there, face to face with fellow humans who were defeated and bleeding. The knights regarded the order as unchivalrous, and they refused it. Thousands of French soldiers were allowed to go home.

Henry's cold-blooded decision to massacre was not triggered by aggression, any more than was the decision five centuries later in 1915 by the British High Command – also at a safe distance from the battlefield – that it was worth risking 10,000 casualties a day to break through the German lines in the Somme. It was cold logic that dictated the bloodiest battle in human history, which left 1,200,000 dead and injured – and failed in its objectives.

As so often happens, the ordinary soldier bore no ill will towards the enemy, recognising that they were doing a job just like he was. Soldiers going home on leave were often surprised at how vehemently the folks at home hated the Germans. At times, when the trenches were within hailing distance, officers had a difficult job discouraging fraternisation. Between bombard-ments, if somebody managed to bring down a passing partridge, he was allowed to retrieve it from no man's land.

We are instinctively co-operative creatures, not killers. From our forebears we have also inherited, to use Ardrey's phrase, "many a social nicety". We are not bad animals and, under normal circumstances, get along well enough with one another and with our fellow creatures.

The world is now more urbanised than rural; but we cannot live by urban comforts alone. Just as one steps back to admire a painting, or, the longer one is away the more one appreciates home, so our increasing distance from our hunter-gatherer past lends it enchantment; humanity, newly urbanised, is beginning to appreciate the outdoors, and wanting, more and more often, to "get away from it all", however, far that might be. In my grandfather's day, the countryside began outside the kitchen door. Now, one must at least get on a bus.

The special fascination of the African wilds is that they take us all the way back to the Pleistocene – our starting point, and our habitat for 99% of humankind's existence. It is the enchantment of the African bush, and the way television so marvellously portrays it for those who cannot physically travel there, that is playing a vital role in humanity's growing aesthetic appreciation of Africa – the world's "last big nature reserve" – and our desire to see and conserve what is left.

It came home to me quite forcibly when, in Sumatra, I visited a gallery of art depicting the natural beauty of this tropical region – its enormous leaves, its flamboyant flowers, and its extravagantly beautiful birds; and I realised there was no sky in these paintings. Every painting was filled, top to bottom, with heavy, large-leafed foliage sprinkled with vivid colour. How utterly different from Africa. Central Africa has its tropical jungle and big floppy butterflies; but that's not where our ancestors originated, or where many lived. The open African grassveld – Ardrey's "sky-swept savanna" – was our birthplace. One cannot help but feel a resonance with its open spaces – the overwhelming African skyscape.

I believe the media, and particularly television, has awakened in humans a new sense of wonder and a greater curiosity regarding our animal contemporaries, and a desire to be among them in their own habitat – the habitat in which we evolved. Like television, the World Wide Web and the extraordinary number of natural history books and magazines being published these days are pro-conservation. Even hunting journals are softening their redneck approach, finding it politic to encourage a deeper and more genuine respect for, and knowledge of, nature. These are good signs; and so is the resultant rise of eco-tourism as a leisure pursuit.

Eco-tourism has become a major foreign exchange earner in Africa; but it took the death of a lion to underscore this.

4 To kill a lion

Out of the eater came forth meat,
and out of the strong came forth sweetness.

Samson's riddle in Judges 14:14

Aconservationist must be an optimist, otherwise there's simply no point in being one. But it is not only the optimist in me that makes me dismiss the often-quoted contention that the African lion – currently being poisoned, poached and hunted on an unsustainable scale – will be extinct within 20 years. The situation is indeed dire, but it is not terminal.

Until the 19th century, the African lion was found from Cape Town to the Mediterranean. It lived in deserts, in mountains, in the bush, along the coast – ironically, everywhere except in its legendary "kingdom", the jungle.

Counting lions

Lions are very difficult to count and their numbers, anyway, can fluctuate wildly year by year, depending on the rainfall. In wet years, hunting is difficult; their prey species no longer have to risk drinking at waterholes staked out by the cats. The lions have to work harder and eat less. Cub mortality rises. Some cubs starve; some are killed by adults when trying to feed at a crowded kill. In dry years, because prey species are forced to use waterholes, predation soars and cubs thrive.

Lion numbers have slumped in the last 20 years, some believe by a third, while others say the number has halved.

One estimate was that there were 35,000 left in 2011. Half of that number are likely to disappear over the next two decades, according to the *Proceedings of the National Academy of Sciences* in America, published in October 2015. Who knows? Even now, the number is pitiful for a continent whose icon is the lion. The cat now occupies only 8% of its historical range, and its populations have been extinguished in 12 African states. Four more countries in West Africa might follow, for lions in that region are down to a few hundred and confined to 1% of their former territory.

The fate of the Kenyan lions is typical. A century ago lions were abundant there, and sometimes wandered into Nairobi. The aptly named Scots big-game hunter, J. A. Hunter, was employed around the mid-20th century to reduce lion numbers in the Maasai's territory. Not long before, Maasai cattle had been hard hit by a major rinderpest epidemic, and lions were making short work of the survivors. Hunter used mongrels from the Nairobi dog pound – dogs that would enthusiastically, and often suicidally, rush at the lions and confuse them while the hunter placed his shots. His strategy was for a Maasai assistant to get the dogs to chase a pride of lions into a gully while he waited at the other end for them to emerge. In this way he could shoot as many as seven lions in quick succession. He generally found lions easy to shoot, and killed 88 in three months. Significantly, only 20 of the skins were in prime condition.

Hunter sometimes travelled on the Mombasa/Nairobi line – made notorious by the "man-eaters of Tsavo" at the turn of the century, when scores of railway workers were eaten by a rogue pair. The train driver, if he spotted game ahead, would stop the train to allow Hunter to shoot not only lions beside the track but once, while passengers waited, a fair-sized tusker. Lions were often shot quite casually in those days.

Kenya banned all hunting in 1977, but lion numbers have continued to decline dramatically, along with other populations of charismatic megafauna. The country, once famous for its lions, is nowadays seriously worried about the viability of its lion population – the lowest in its history. Kenya Wildlife Service (KWS) believes the country is down to about 2,000 lions spread over six districts. The main causes are poaching and habitat loss. Nobody ever envisaged Kenya without lions – until now.

It seems that a simple ban on hunting is not the solution.

Just how many lions exist in Tanzania's vast Selous Game Reserve is a matter of hot debate, but it is probably the most populous lion area in Africa. Two estimates in 2012–2013 arrived at figures of 4,300 and 7,644 respectively, with the latter study also claiming that a further 4,953 live in the surrounding protected areas. If this figure is correct, it amounts to 12,597 lions – half Africa's total. One of the studies also noted that the ratio of male to female adult lions was declining – from 1:1.23 in 1997 to 1:3 (one male to three females) in 2009. The reason is clear enough: 80% of the Selous is open to hunters, who shoot too many males; a phenomenon that has been noted in other hunting areas.

Tanzania's 30,000 square kilometre Serengeti National Park claims to have almost as many lions as the Selous – 4,000. The park is famous for its annual wildebeest migration, when 1,500,000 of these animals move like a tide across the plain and leap en masse into a steep-sided crocodile-infested river – dogged by predators. The next-door Maasai Mara in Kenya is half the size (15,000 square kilometres) and has only about 800 lions – not far off half of Kenya's total.

There are now, according to most sources, between 20,000 and 25,000 lions in the whole of Africa – all are confined to the sub-Saharan region. Most live in and around protected areas.

Africa's national parks, game reserves and other protected landscapes are essential to the species' survival. Although protected on paper, many parks are vulnerable to the same anthropogenic threats that occur in human-dominated landscapes outside their boundaries. The lion is now totally dependent on humankind for its conservation; I suppose everything is.

African lions are classified as "Vulnerable to extinction" on the International Union for Conservation of Nature's (IUCN) Red List of Threatened Species. However, the lions of West Africa are considered "Critically Endangered" (a rating one stop short of extinct). Lions in this region have lost nearly 99% of their historical range, and only 400 remain.

Some of the African countries that allow lion hunting have begun taking action to safeguard populations, heeding the scientific consensus that poorly managed hunting is unsustainable. In recent years Mozambique, Tanzania, Zambia and Zimbabwe have enacted significant reforms regarding lion hunting practices, including reducing their quotas for lions. At different times, both Zambia and Zimbabwe have suspended lion hunting for years to allow populations to recover.

However, lion populations in much of Africa are in freefall. Only in four countries, all in southern Africa, is the trend in the opposite direction: Botswana, Namibia, South Africa and Zimbabwe. Together they are home to an estimated 24–33% of Africa's lions. Here, lion numbers have increased by 12% over the past 20 years, but much of this gain, especially in South Africa, is the result of reintroductions into fenced, intensively managed and relatively well-funded reserves – a scenario not replicable for most of the remaining lion range. The gains in southern Africa obscure the rates of decline elsewhere.

Only six countries are known to harbour more than 1,000 wild lions: Tanzania and Kenya in East Africa, and Botswana,

Mozambique, South Africa, and Zimbabwe in southern Africa. A seventh country, Zambia, may contain close to that number.

Ten areas are considered to be "lion strongholds" (with populations containing at least 500 adults) in Africa. Several of these span international borders. They are Ruaha-Rungwa, Serengeti-Mara and Tsavo-Mkomazi in Kenya/Tanzania, Selous in Tanzania, Luangwa in Zambia, Kgalagadi in Botswana/South Africa, Okavango-Hwange in Zimbabwe/Botswana, Mid-Zambezi in Mozambique/Zambia/Zimbabwe, Niassa in Mozambique, and Great Limpopo in Mozambique/South Africa/Zimbabwe.

In Angola, Central African Republic, Somalia and South Sudan, civil conflict and poorly funded, ill-maintained protected areas are believed to have driven lion populations into a steep decline.

It's difficult to estimate lion losses, because poaching, conflict-killing (to protect livestock and human lives) and other illegal killings are likely to be more prevalent in the areas with weak monitoring, where statistics are least reliable. Many lion deaths are never recorded. One conference estimated that "Taking all factors into account, the number of lions killed illegally across Africa is easily five times the number killed by trophy hunters, and it may be up to 10 times as high in some populations".

There are eight countries that consistently export lion trophies: Zimbabwe, Tanzania, South Africa, Botswana, Central African Republic, Mozambique, Namibia and Zambia.

The killing of Cecil

If lions do survive into the next century and beyond, as I believe they will, then we can look back to 1 July 2015 as the day their future brightened. That was the day Walter Palmer, a middle-aged dentist with a practice in Bloomington, Minnesota, and led by Theo Bronkhorst, a South African professional hunter, shot a magnificent black-maned lion. Some reports said a carcass was used to lure the lion out of Zimbabwe's Hwange National Park; but Hwange's lions often wander outside the park's boundaries. Once the lion was in the privately owned Gwaai Concession, Palmer shot it with a crossbow powerful enough to fell an elephant. The bolt, striking somewhat off target, merely wounded the lion; so according to the hunter's code of ethics, Palmer was obliged to follow it up. It took a day to track the wounded animal, which was then killed using a rifle. Palmer and Bronkhorst then posed, grinning triumphantly, to be photographed next to its corpse – with the crossbow. The deed itself outraged many across the world, but the widely published photograph and the dumb pride in the hunters' faces unsurprisingly hit a raw nerve among conservationists and the wider public.

For the white-male-dominated big-game hunting industry, it was a public relations disaster.

Palmer paid $50,000 for his hunt, which appears to have been legal in terms of Zimbabwean law. His real problem, though, was that this particular 13-year-old lion happened to be a favourite among tourists. Cecil was everything that a tourist expected of the "King of the Jungle". Thousands of overseas visitors treasure the pictures they took of this particularly handsome black-maned male, who was unfazed by safari vehicles and the clicking of cameras. He was wearing a barely visible GPS tracking collar, as part of a research project by the University of Oxford's Wildlife Conservation Research Unit (WildCru) dating back to 2009.

The fact that a man could take pleasure in killing him, purely to decorate a wall in some Minnesota city, drew little admiration anywhere outside Safari Club International, the international hunters' association.

The global response

Worldwide, animal lovers and conservationists, scientists, presidents and prime ministers, film stars and schoolchildren spontaneously voiced their disgust. So vociferous and prolonged was the protest that, to demonstrate their concern, countries from America to the Far East took swift actions regarding the future handling of hunting trophies. France and Holland banned the importing of lion parts outright, and Britain announced it was considering a similar move in 2017.

The United Nations General Assembly adopted a non-binding resolution to strengthen conservation efforts, and Germany's UN Ambassador, Harald Braun, linked the resolution to the killing, saying, "Like most people in the world, we are outraged".

This universal condemnation of the "hunt" was unprecedented – a conservation landmark. It indicated a growing awareness of the lion's slide towards extinction.

The Cecil episode brought to mind Samson's riddle in the Old Testament – "out of the strong came forth sweetness" – a riddle prompted by the sight of honeybees nesting inside a dead lion's ribcage. Good came from Cecil's death. A lot of good.

Until Cecil's death, most people around the world had taken for granted that the lion was a permanent part of the African scene, as iconic as Kilimanjaro, as picturesque as the Victoria Falls, as distinctive as Table Mountain. For tourists, it was an essential part of the African experience. Few realised that the lion population had dropped so low.

The killing of Cecil brought immediate reactions from the governments of the United States, Canada, and the European Union – there was a move to ban lion trophies entering France and, soon afterwards, Holland. Australia announced similar measures. An anti-hunting fervour swept across America. Palmer's home and dental practice were picketed for days by angry people. Palmer had to close down his practice for weeks, and a year later was publicly regretting the incident.

A US Congress spokesperson on international conservation, Betty McCollum, called for an investigation of Palmer and of the killing.

The Oxford research team that had been tracking Cecil released pictures of the lion, which were published around the world, and even projected onto the Empire State Building in New York.

It was an extraordinary episode.

The public outrage at the Cecil affair soon attracted the attention of lawmakers. US Senator Bob Menendez, with support from other senators, introduced tougher laws regarding animal trophies, specifically mentioning Cecil and stalling Palmer's hopes of bringing Cecil's head into America.

Coincidentally the USA, at the time, had scheduled an announcement regarding the suspension of import permits for hunters bringing in elephant trophies from Tanzania and Zimbabwe. It declared that trophy hunting of elephants was not sustainable, nor was it contributing to conservation. It cited "questionable management practices (in the countries concerned) and a lack of effective law enforcement and weak governance". The conservationists – professional and amateur – lost no time in pointing out that the same applied to lions. As a result of the Cecil furore, the United States Fish and Wildlife Service (FWS) added the African lion to its endangered species list. US President Barack Obama personally announced a tightening of laws controlling the import of hunting trophies in general. In effect, every lion trophy, henceforth, had to be certified as coming from a country with a stable government and a responsible conservation management system in place, as well as a policy for safeguarding the lion's status in the wild. South Africa and Namibia are about the only countries in Africa that comply. Botswana could also have met these conditions, but in 2015 it banned big-game hunting altogether.

A year after the Cecil killing, Zimbabwe recorded a huge drop in its hunting season bookings – 70% down at one point. American and European Union hunters were staying away partly because bringing hunting trophies home promised to be a bureaucratic nightmare. Dan Ashe, head of the US Fish and Wildlife Service (FWS), was quoted in the New York-based *Huffington Post* in October 2016 saying, "(We) cannot and will not allow trophies into the US from any nation whose lion conservation programme fails to meet key criteria for transparency, scientific management and effectiveness ... In the case of lions taken from captive populations in South Africa, that burden of proof has not been met".

Critics saw a loophole in this policy: the regulations were such that hunters need only prove that revenue from the hunt – whether captive or wild – went directly towards conservation in that country. In other words, a generous cheque to the conservation authorities might be enough to do the trick. With the swing to the right in American politics that occurred a month later, there were fears that the new administration would prove more sympathetic towards the largely right-wing hunting lobby.

The European Union, like the USA, had already tightened regulations prohibiting the import of lion trophies, though at first only from certain West African countries where lions are very near extinction. The British government reaffirmed its position on the illegal wildlife trade, saying the importation of lion trophies would cease from 2017.

By mid-August, eight weeks after the Cecil episode, 42 airlines had announced they would no longer carry big-game trophies – namely, lion, leopard, elephant, rhinoceros and buffalo – joining British Airways and Virgin Atlantic, which already had such bans in place.

Activists called for a ban on bow hunting, lion baiting, and hunting from hides (blinds).

Safari Club International, a hunters' association that encourages competition among its members to see who can assemble the widest variety of African trophy heads, suspended both Palmer's and Bronkhorst's memberships. It stated, "those who intentionally take wildlife illegally should be prosecuted and punished to the maximum extent allowed by law". (It was wrongly thought for a time that the hunt had been illegal in Zimbabwe.)

The late-night talk-show host Jimmy Kimmel helped raise $150,000 in donations in less than 24 hours to aid WildCru, the institute that had been tracking Cecil's activity.

The Chinese response was more ambiguous.

Two months after the Cecil episode, the Botswana-based conservation journalist Oscar Nkala reported from Harare that "the killing of Cecil the lion has sparked a flurry of Chinese aid to protect wildlife in the country". Although China was not involved in the Cecil affair, it has been heavily implicated in Africa's massive loss of lions. For years, it had been totally indifferent to the fate of Africa's lions even though (thanks to its thriving market for lion bones) it was the importer of 90% of those killed by its own and Vietnamese crime syndicates.

In December 2016, 18 months after Cecil's death, Nkala reported on a ceremony in Hwange National Park when the new Chinese ambassador to Zimbabwe, Huang Ping, handed over millions of dollars' worth of four-wheel drive vehicles, tractors, pick-ups, graders and dump trucks. The equipment was promised before Cecil was shot, but Cecil had now become the world's focal point regarding the plight of African wildlife, even overshadowing the poisoning of 300 elephants in Hwange National Park.

Yet even as the ambassador was pledging to help rescue Zimbabwe's wildlife situation, customs officers at Harare

Airport arrested a Chinese businessman with crates containing 10 spotted hyenas and a lion bound for a Chinese safari park – all without permits, all in a pitiable condition, and all from Hwange National Park.

Zimbabwe Conservation Task Force (ZCTF) chairman Johnny Rodrigues accused China of "decimating the country's wildlife" and disclosed that more hyenas and lions as well as buffalo and elephant were in bomas in the Mtshibi section of the Hwange National Park and awaiting export to China, apparently with government blessing.

African indifference

Among African governments, the initial reaction to the Cecil episode was largely one of indifference. Gabon's Foreign Minister Emmanuel Issoze-Ngondet – whose heavily forested country is one of the more enlightened in Africa when it comes to conservation – did say that Cecil's killing was "a matter of deep concern for all countries in Africa". But this claim seemed vacuous in view of media reports suggesting that practically all Africans – including those living around Hwange National Park – could not have cared less. The rural population has long regarded lions as vermin. Many see no value whatsoever in a predator that kills their cattle, and sometimes their neighbours. They perceive no economic use for live lions, and would like to see them exterminated. Elephants too. And rhino.

Sarel van der Merwe, chairman of the African Lion Working Group which is affiliated with the Cat and Conservation Breeding Specialist Groups in the IUCN Species Survival Commission, talked to a man in the Omo valley in Ethiopia about the decline in wild animal numbers. The man said, "Today the hunters find far fewer animals, and a kind of silence waits in the bush. But I won't say it's bad. Fools and white men may miss the lion". Asked if the ancestors would be angered by his indifference, he said, "What can they do? I've got nothing".

Official comments mirrored the public's views. Zimbabwe's acting information minister, Prisca Mupfumira, when questioned days after Cecil's killing, asked "What lion?" Presumably she had become aware of Cecil by the time when, 15 months later, the Safari Operators Association of Zimbabwe reported a serious decline in the hunting industry. Its chairman, Emmanuel Fundira, said, "There was one client who offered us a ridiculous amount of money to come and shoot Jericho, Cecil's brother". Fundira was worried about the loss of income – "We can do almost nothing to protect wildlife without revenue from hunting". This is a point of view that cannot be ignored, and to which we shall return.

The government-controlled *Chronicle* in Harare commented: "It is not an overstatement that almost 99.99% of Zimbabweans didn't know about this animal ... we have just learned, thanks to the British media, that we had Africa's most famous lion all along, an icon!"

Jean Kapata, Zambia's minister of tourism, said "In Africa, a human being is more important than an animal. I don't know about the Western world", suggesting that the West seemed more concerned with the welfare of a lion in Zimbabwe than with that of Africans themselves.

South Africa's President Jacob Zuma was equally dismissive: "What it sounds like from a distance is that the hunter did not know that Cecil was so popular, just saw a lion, and killed a lion, and it's Cecil, and Cecil is very well loved and it caused a problem, because everyone wants to go and see Cecil. I think it's just an incident."

Yet the Gabonese minister's remarks proved prescient, as the loss of hunting revenue soon forced Africa to take the

Cecil phenomenon seriously. Just before the anniversary of Cecil's death, 28 African lion-range states got together in Entebbe at a conference titled *Beyond Cecil*. Seventy-one delegates attended. And, weeks later, WildCru hosted the *Cecil Summit* in Oxford, gathering 58 scientists and other professionals to brainstorm the lion situation. The ghost of Cecil loomed large.

Paul Funston, an internationally recognised large-carnivore biologist who heads Panthera's Lion and Cheetah programme, said in a paper titled *Beyond Cecil: Africa's Lions in Crisis*: "... with the loss of Cecil, the world responded unequivocally that it stands with Africa in saving the lion. Sadly, we have since lost hundreds and possibly thousands of lions. The species is now approaching the point of no return in many countries. Saving this extraordinary animal requires the international community to convert their outrage over Cecil into action and dollars supporting African governments, people and initiatives fighting to save the lion."

Canned hunting

Unexpectedly, a lot of the opprobrium following the Cecil episode was directed at South Africa rather than Zimbabwe. The spotlight fell on South Africa's infamous "canned hunting" industry. There are probably around 200 privately owned lion-breeding farms in South Africa that allow would-be hunters to safely shoot specially bred "trophy" lions. The captive lions – there were about 6,000 of them in 2016 – are handfed and never go into the wild until the day they are released into a confined area of bush to be shot. "Hunting" is hardly involved but, annually, hundreds of tourists take lions' heads home, presumably claiming they were shot on safari. The remains – especially the skeletons – are sold to Far Eastern buyers. In 2013 a complete skeleton was fetching $2,100.

Lionesses are often raised and slaughtered just for their bones.

Shortly before the Cecil incident, Peter Borchert, the South African publisher and editor of the wildlife magazine, *Africa Geographic*, and a widely respected voice among professional conservationists, wrote a much-circulated post on the online news service, *Daily Maverick*:

"In South Africa there are some 10,000 lions and the numbers are increasing all the time. A conservation success, some might aver. But the lie behind this statistic is revealed in the fact that South Africa is the only lion-range state that has three separate classifications for these great cats: captive, managed and wild. And so we find that only 3,000 – less than a third – are truly wild and living in designated conservation areas.

"The rest, 7,000 or so, live on private farms, mostly in small crowded camps where their social structure is destroyed, not to mention their genetic integrity. The only purpose, despite rather weak attempts to justify the activity as conservation-based or 'scientific,' is to breed them.

"Young cubs are great drawcards for visitors, especially if they can pet them. Slightly older, they provide a rush for visitors who pay to walk with them in the veld. And finally, as they grow into the magnificence of adulthood, with flowing manes and faces unblemished, they become handsome targets for trophy hunters. Hundreds more are slaughtered and shipped to the East for the burgeoning lion bone trade."

Borchert described the canned lion industry as "a cynical and highly profitable niche industry (which) enjoys a powerful lobby in high places".

A canned lion hunt in South Africa costs a great deal less than a legitimate "fair chase" hunt – around $20,000 as against, say, $80,000. However, Jacalyn Beales, an animal welfare advocate in Toronto who founded PACH (People Against Canned Hunting), says the canned lion industry is so popular in South Africa that in 2012 it generated approximately US$70 million, which was then worth well over R1 billion.

In 2015, the wildlife campaigner Ian Michler launched a documentary exposing the brutality of the canned lion industry. He'd been calling for its demise for years. The film, *Blood Lions,* shocked audiences wherever it was shown, and severely tarnished South Africa's reputation. It revealed the cynicism of an industry that, as Michler said, "thrives on greed and blood lust". One depressing sequence showed what can only be described as a pitiful "herd" of listless male lions sluggishly moving about in a bare prison-of-war style enclosure. Each lion is kept until ready to be released into an area of natural bush where the "hunter" can easily find it and shoot it. Hunters are told not to shoot the lion in the head, because that spoils the trophy. This means that one shot is generally insufficient. A marksman is there to finish the job.

It's a horrible business and it appeals, mostly, to the insensitive. According to psychologists, these "big-game hunters" are not trying to do something macho in order to impress women – most women are repulsed by it all – but to impress the boys back home.

Farms offering captive hunting gain a lot of revenue by advertising overseas for young conservation-minded "volunteers" who, at a price, can spend their days cuddling and playing with lion cubs and helping feed them. Older volunteers can have their photographs taken while they walk with friendly sub-adult lions. All are told they are helping to bring up lions that are destined to be released into the wild. Few know that once the lion is fully grown, and by now totally trusting of humans, it will be executed by foreigners who will pay thousands of dollars to take its head home. The farmers claim their farms are part of the safari-hunting industry. But that's like prostitutes boasting of their economic contribution to the hospitality industry.

The South African backlash

The South African public's wrath, as information regarding canned hunting was published, was as heated as that from outside the country. The domestic reaction was further stoked by the exposure of a Free State game farmer who allowed tourists to sit next to his circular perimeter fence while his staff rounded up farm-reared antelope of various species and stampeded them along the fence so that clients could take potshots.

The Professional Hunters' Association of South Africa (PHASA) was severely embarrassed by the Cecil affair and by the canned hunting publicity. It had only itself to blame. The association had publicly condemned canned hunting as long ago as 2004, but had done little, if anything, to stop it. In 2014, PHASA again condemned canned hunting at the 7th African Wildlife Consultative Forum in Windhoek, Namibia. But that same year the South African Department of Environmental Affairs, backed by PHASA's president, Hermann Meyeridricks, tried to persuade Australia's environment minister, Greg Hunt, to reconsider his proposal to ban the import of lion trophies. Hunt was unmoved. "It's not fair, it's not humane, it's not 21st century. On my watch it's not acceptable," he said. The ban was finalised in 2015.

About 4,000 lions were then in "captive breeding" in South Africa. In 2014, according to the UK arm of one of the most persistent lobby groups, the Campaign Against Canned Hunting (CACH), there were 64 demonstrations worldwide, protesting South Africa's lenient attitude towards captive lion hunting. Of 11 international petitions targeting canned hunting, one attracted almost 2 million signatures. Yet by 2016, despite at least 10 international and national campaigns against it, the number of captive lions had increased by 50%.

In 2016, Andrew Venter, CEO of the Wildlands Conservation Trust, who was driving a motion at the International Union for

Conservation of Nature (IUCN) conference in Hawaii to end trophy hunting, told the congress that 1,000 lions were shot legally in South Africa in 2015 – but 990 were captive. The majority were shot by Americans; the rest by Germans, Spaniards, Canadians and Danes. As regards the trophy trade, Laos, Vietnam, the United States and Spain are the main buyers of legal lion parts. They are mostly interested in head-and-shoulders trophies, skins and whole carcasses.

Are canned lions saving wild ones?

Some hunters and wildlife conservationists argue that canned hunting can help conserve lions, and that similar methods can even be applied to boost numbers of other endangered species. They claim that for every captive lion killed, a wild lion is saved. Even the Smithsonian Conservation Biology Institute, quoted by Jacalyn Beales, appears to back this, suggesting that "establishing captive populations for saving species from extinction is an important contribution ... to conservation." However, Beales refutes the notion that captive-bred lions are helping to take pressure off the wild population. There's a huge difference between hunting a wild lion and a "canned" one. A wild lion must be tracked for hours and might ambush its pursuer; indeed, lions still account for the majority of deaths in the field among big-game hunters – though, thanks to the power and accuracy of the modern hunting rifle, such deaths are nowadays rare occurrences. The captive lion, on the other hand, is docile, perhaps even tame, and may be half-drugged when it is hunted. It seems highly unlikely either that a "real" big-game hunter would be interested in shooting a "canned" lion, or that a person who is prepared to shoot a captive lion would have the courage to hunt a wild one – even assuming they could afford the fees. So instead of absorbing the demand for lions to kill, the canned hunting industry has simply created a demand from a new and not terribly admirable market sector.

Ethical hunting

There is nevertheless a case for ethical hunting that must be seriously considered.

PHASA's spokesman, Tharia Urwin, while stating that ethical hunters were as concerned about the welfare of lions as were animal-rights activists – which, for quite different reasons, they are – has warned against banning trophy hunting holus-bolus. PHASA pointed out that ethical trophy hunting contributed R1.8 billion to South Africa's GDP and directly benefited several communities.

In Africa generally, it creates economic incentives for the retention of large areas of state, community and private land for wildlife. Where the economic benefits from hunting are retained locally, it provides incentives for communities to coexist with wildlife. In some wildlife areas, hunters contribute to anti-poaching measures and help prevent human encroachment. Trophy hunting can operate in areas of low infrastructure or low scenic appeal, and even under conditions of political instability where regular tourism is generally not viable. Hunters claim they target only post-reproductive males (but how on earth can they tell?).

Regarding the cruelty aspect, professional hunters argue that death from a bullet – assuming it is well placed – is instantaneous. This is true. I witnessed, as an observer one night, the culling of 160 surplus impala using a spotlight and a silenced high-velocity .22 rifle. Each animal, blinded by the spotlight, died instantly; and the meat was sold at cost to communities beyond the fence. As a meat eater, I had to admit that the death of a hunter's quarry is far less traumatic than the fate of a cow destined for the abattoir. There is no way I could stomach watching the slaughter of a cow or sheep for my supper, or for my belt or shoes. It would therefore be hypocritical of me to condemn ethical hunting on humane grounds.

Trophy hunting in itself removes relatively few lions from the population, but it can pose an added threat when that population is already under intense pressure from people. Unlike many ungulate species, which have evolved with high rates of natural predation, lions are highly vulnerable to overhunting. The lion's social system elevates this vulnerability: removal of pride males can cause disruption within a population, driving increased rates of infanticide, lowering reproductive and survival rates, and displacing pride members into higher-risk areas. Trophy hunting is often carried out on the boundaries of national parks, siphoning off lions (like Cecil) from protected populations.

The revenues that hunting generates may not be fairly distributed. Government agencies that collect the revenues may become dependent on them, and thus incentivised both to keep quotas high and to retain the revenues (whether for reasons of bureaucracy or corruption) rather than share them with the affected communities and individuals. As a result, funds are often not adequate for managing and securing lands effectively.

Deciding on a set of ethics for lion hunting is not as easy as it might seem. The most difficult question is: how big must a hunting area be before it can offer ethical hunting? How big must it be before a hunter can say he set off in fair pursuit and that the lion had a chance of escape? Obviously, to confine a lion to, say, 50 hectares and then invite visitors to "hunt it" would be outrageous. But what about 6,000 hectares? In southern Africa, judging by advertisements in hunting magazines, this would be considered a fair-sized hunting region. But effectively the animal is still trapped.

Poisoning and "revenge killings"

In some parts of Africa, lions pose a danger to livestock and even sometimes to humans. For a herder dependent on just a few cattle or goats, a single livestock loss can be devastating. The psychological impacts, including feelings of resentment, are also significant: many of those who live in close proximity to wild lions have a negative perception of the animals, regarding them as vermin that should be eradicated. Although poisoning of wildlife is illegal in most African countries, it is poorly policed and prosecuted, and extremely difficult to control. The widespread availability of both cheap, highly toxic pesticides and herbicides has provided an effective tool for killing lions.

Poaching

Trophy hunting and poisoning, controversial though they may be, are by no means the greatest threats to Africa's lions. Lions are poached for their body parts, which are used for ceremonies and rituals, and as medicine, decorations and talismans in many African nations, including Somalia, Nigeria, Benin, Burkina Faso, Kenya, Senegal and Cameroon. One investigation uncovered the use of lions in traditional medicine in Nigeria, where their fat, meat, bones, teeth, lungs, skin, eyes, heart and liver are used to treat a variety of ailments. Cameroon's government identified the trade in skins "as a major cause of the decline in lion populations in western and central Africa." But by far the greatest danger to lions is posed by the bone export market.

Lion bones

If lion, elephant and rhino do indeed become extinct in the wilds it will not be due to disciplined hunting; it will be due to poaching, and the naivety of the northern hemisphere. Far Eastern criminal syndicates are recruiting impoverished Africans to supply animal parts for absurd medical or aphrodisiacal reasons. They are offering rewards that jobless rural Africans find hard to resist.

At one time, the Far East paid huge prices for tiger bones, which were reduced to powder and then mixed with wine. This "tiger wine" was claimed to relieve arthritis, enhance libido and strengthen the drinker's own bones. However, by 2016 this thriving market had helped reduce the world's wild tiger population to an estimated 3,890, and tiger bones had become scarce.

China, Vietnam and, to a lesser extent, Thailand – all signatories to CITES – having nearly extinguished their own tigers, have turned to Africa for a substitute. Presumably they have managed to convince the consumers back home that lion bones, when powdered into wine, have the same medicinal power as tiger bones – which, of course, is true enough; both have the same therapeutic properties as powdered crockery or old socks. Nevertheless, the market for lion bones in 2015 and 2016 became voracious. Far Eastern consumers were paying $500 a bottle for the stuff.

The two post-Cecil gatherings – *Beyond Cecil* and *The Cecil Summit* – noted that the growing trade in lion bones and other body parts was a new threat to the survival of wild lions.

The subject loomed large at the 17th Conference of the Parties (CoP17) of the Convention on International Trade in Endangered Species (CITES) in Johannesburg in September 2016. The "parties" – the 147 participating nations – surprisingly voted against a proposal to establish a zero annual export quota for wild lion bones, claws and teeth. The conservation lobby had hoped that lions would be transferred from Appendix II (which allows for limited commercial exploitation) to Appendix I (full protection), thus prohibiting any international commercial trade in lions or lion parts.

But the CITES delegates voted for a compromise. This allowed South Africa, the only country that is openly trading in lion parts, to continue to do so; but it was now obliged to establish annual export quotas – including from its captive breeding operations. And it had to report annually to CITES.

Jeffrey Flocken, North American Regional Director at IFAW (International Fund for Animal Welfare), commenting on the CITES decision, said, "Whilst not a victory (for conservation) it is an incremental step forward that we hope will lead to greater protection for lions". John Scanlon, Secretary-General of CITES, was more sanguine: he thought the conference was "a game changer that will be remembered as a point in history when the tide turned in favour of ensuring the survival of our most vulnerable wildlife".

In the context of the lion's survival, the CITES decision was as negative as it was unexpected. A week after the conference, the freelance travel writer and explorer Don Pinnock reported a wildlife poisoning incident in Mozambique's Limpopo National Park next to Kruger Park. A research team discovered the bodies of two nyala, a warthog and an impala laced with poison. Lying nearby were the targets – two dead lions. Their bones had been removed. The poisoning also cost the lives of 51 vultures (their heads removed for *muti* – traditional medicine), three fish eagles, a yellow-billed kite and a giant eagle-owl. Such are the consequences of the trade in lion parts.

Leon Marshall, of *National Geographic*, one of Africa's veteran conservation journalists, foresaw all this in 2010 when he wrote about the lion bone trade:

"At the moment merchants are mostly getting their supplies under government permit from hunting farms on which captive-bred lions are released to be shot as trophies – itself a rather grotesque business. One of the concerns, however, is that as the trade grows, it could lead to already endangered lion populations in the wild getting poached for their bones. Another worry is that it could serve as further encouragement to the commercial lion-breeding industry which the government is trying to curb, not least because of the bad image it creates of a country that has tourism, particularly nature tourism, as its fastest growing industry. The trend adds to an already grim picture in which animal species in South Africa are under threat from poachers cashing in on enduring primitive beliefs that the physical attributes of animals can be acquired by ingesting their body parts."

Asian consumers apparently pay more for bones from free-ranging lions, believing the effects are more potent. But who can tell the difference between the bones of captive lions and those of wild lions? As long as it is legal to sell lion bones, it is easy to launder parts from wild lions and export them using the same trade routes. Thus, the pressure on lions may continue until CoP18.

In 2016, the South African National Biodiversity Institute (SANBI) recommended an 800-skeleton annual quota for this perfectly silly market. Sanbi sees its mission as "exploring, revealing, celebrating, and championing biodiversity for the benefit and enjoyment of all South Africans". How much South Africans will enjoy exporting 800 lion skeletons a year remains to be seen.

Southern Africa has serious problems with lion poaching. As in most of Africa, corruption at almost every level is sabotaging national conservation goals. In 2015, the investigative environmentalist journalist Fiona Macleod of the Johannes-burg-based *Mail & Guardian* found that South African farmers were, with impunity, using cattle-rustling routes in the remote, semi-arid Northern Cape to smuggle wild lions and other predators out of Botswana to supply the growing demand for lion-bone potions in the Far East.

She found the illicit trade, organised by cartels, was adding to the pressures "that could see the extinction of big cats in the wild within 10 to 12 years". South Africa's government was showing little interest, she averred. The Environment Minister, Edna Molewa, told parliament a moratorium was unnecessary "because they do not pose a threat to the survival of the species in the wild". Nobody mentioned the morality of aiding and abetting China's fraudulent medicine industry.

Dereck Joubert, leader of *National Geographic*'s Big Cats Initiative, who has researched and filmed predators in Botswana for more than 25 years, believes the opposite. He said the lion-bone market was adding to the "emergency situation" facing all Africa's wild lions. Macleod quotes him as saying, "The bone trade out of South Africa, nearly all from captive-bred lions, is stimulating the market in Asia, which is far bigger than the supply will ever be. Selling lion bones on the market is also putting more pressure on Asia's tiger populations, and there are fewer than 3,000 tigers left in the wild."

Macleod says several South Africans were allocated land in communal farming areas in southern Botswana, and some owned farms on the South African side of the border in the Northern Cape. "The smuggling routes they set up around the McCarthy's Rest border post, about 200 kilometres north of Kuruman, are now being used to supply live lions (from Botswana) to captive breeding facilities in South Africa, which are making a killing from selling lion bones as a substitute for tiger bones in traditional Asian potions".

Farmers are employing cattle rustlers and old cattle-rustling routes to "launder" the live predators across the border. Macleod was told that "often they are cubs taken from lactating females, who are lured out of the Kgalagadi Transfrontier Park to watering points in the arid region and killed (by) specialised capture teams supplied with vehicles and other equipment by the buyers in South Africa. Cheetah, leopard, hyena and ivory are also part of the cross-border contraband". She was told that the details of the smuggling had been supplied to police and conservation officials on both sides of the border and although a few arrests had been made, "there was little follow-through because local politicians and authorities in both countries are implicated. There is little interest in stopping even the cattle smuggling, despite the serious threat of foot-and-mouth disease which could affect beef exports".

Questions sent by the *Mail & Guardian* to South Africa's Department of Environmental Affairs and to Botswana's wildlife authorities went unanswered.

When lion bones can sell for thousands of dollars – in 2016, Macleod was told that a complete skeleton was fetching R80,000 ($5,700) – the temptation to poach lions is difficult to resist for Africa's poverty-stricken rural dwellers, who have no love for lions anyway. Even as I write, people living in the hunting area where Cecil was shot are digging up sites where they recall seeing hunting parties burying the remains of shot lions after removing the head, skin and claws. The only hope is that the market for lion bones, which was expanding in 2016, can be curbed quickly enough at the receiving end – China and Vietnam.

The Chinese President, Xi Jinping, made a state visit to Africa in 2015. Rather belatedly, he undertook that his country would accept its responsibility for curbing illicit trading in wild animals and wildlife parts. Judging by figures tabled at the IUCN's 2016 Johannesburg conference, this undertaking had no discernible effect, which is hardly surprising given the volumes and the vested interests involved. According to the African Wildlife Foundation (AWF), a lot of the contraband was entering through Hong Kong; the port handles 60,000 cargo crates a day, of which authorities can examine only 1%.

But according to the AWF there were signs that China was sincere in its efforts to limit illicit wildlife imports. By 2016, it had placed posters along main thoroughfares aimed at disabusing its populace regarding the supposed medicinal benefits of consuming wildlife products, such as lion-bone wine, and it was using the media to explain the threats to Africa's biodiversity and its economy.

Controlling the Chinese wildlife trade might prove a bit like turning a supertanker around. And there's Vietnam to consider. As we shall see in the next chapter, Vietnam shows great reluctance to tackle its wildlife crooks, whose tentacles reach high into government. Undercover agents, giving evidence at the Peace Palace in The Hague, told the Wildlife Justice Commission (WJC) that Vietnam was a huge receiver of illicit wildlife parts; and how easy it was, even in 2016, to smuggle goods across the river to China.

If the Chinese government's controls do prove effective, and if Vietnam can be persuaded to clean up its act, then a decisive step will have been taken towards ensuring the survival of Africa's wild lion population, and its wildlife in general. Defending protected areas could become much less expensive. No more of the night and day helicopter patrols which are wrecking the bush experience for many tourists. No more need for special duty rangers to be trained and deployed as paramilitary personnel.

The African tiger trade

Curiously enough, South Africa is also a notable exporter of tigers, which occur nowhere in Africa except on a tiger-breeding farm in the Karoo. CITES' trade records show that the country exported 131 live Asian tigers over the 11 years up to 2010. Of these, 54 went to the Emirates and 16 to Vietnam; 28 went to

Botswana, which for reasons unknown sent 11 of them back. CITES classifies captive-bred species differently from those in the wild so that the tigers in question, being captive, merely needed export permits. Pieter Kat, director of Lion Aid, a conservation organisation based in Britain, said, "The Arab Emirates is a well-known staging point for the illegal trade of wildlife from Africa, and any live tiger sent to Vietnam will end up in an Asian traditional medicine pot".

Bushmeat hunting

Bushmeat hunting – most of it illegal and uncontrolled – is another major threat to lion survival. Large ungulates on which lions have relied for millennia, such as wildebeest, zebra, buffalo and impala, have been severely depleted, including those in the Serengeti where tens of thousands of wildebeest are killed in snares each year. And the collateral damage is not limited to the lion's diet. Across Africa, lions are often caught and killed in the snares set for antelope, and snares reportedly cause 52% of lion mortalities in Mozambique's Niassa National Reserve.

In some parts, *nyama* (bushmeat) is sold commercially in urban markets, and even to markets in the United States and Europe. An estimated 5 tonnes a week is shipped to Paris. On the local level, bushmeat offers a cheap source of protein for rural populations. The UK-based Born Free Foundation says increasing demand and profitability has meant hunters killing ever greater numbers of wildlife. "Much of this hunting is illegal and the bushmeat trade is now threatening the survival of many wild animals. Indeed, the bushmeat trade is now the single biggest threat facing many wild animal species."

It found 25% of all meat on the market in Nairobi – despite being marked "goat" or "beef" – is from poached animals, and sells at around half the price of lamb or beef. In rural

Mozambique, it costs US$3–4 to buy a chicken, and just US$1.60 for a medium portion of bushmeat.

In Central and West African forests, bushmeat is seen as critical to food security, and this has resulted in the lions losing out almost to the point of extinction. After many thousands of years, humans are once more competing with lions for food.

In most areas, including many protected areas, the level of bushmeat trade, according to the Born Free Foundation, is "generally unsustainable". It told the Entebbe meeting – *Beyond Cecil* – that bushmeat is a "potentially sustainable source of protein if properly regulated. It would, and should, be a by-product of any game reserve if one accepts that conservation is 'the wise use of a natural resource'". But so unrestrained is the trade that giraffe are now being killed for bushmeat and their numbers, Africa-wide, are down to between 80,000 and 110,000.

The good news, according to the Born Free Foundation, was that "there are solutions to most of these threats. Wherever human pressures have been reduced, savanna habitats, their wildlife populations, and particularly lions, have bounced back ... but urgency is needed to mobilise an effective protection and management system for protected areas".

A big threat to the future of the lion in Kenya and Tanzania is retaliatory killing when lions attack livestock. Around the Serengeti, for instance, the Maasai respect the lions (so beloved by tourists) that roam the plains of the reserve, but spear them when they step outside and threaten their herds.

The Entebbe delegates agreed that reducing the vulnerability of livestock to lion predation, and encouraging local people to value the presence of lions, were "critical steps forward to implement effective reform". Funding needs can be reduced if communities are brought on side and effectively engaged in conservation efforts. There is a need, it was said, to "urgently mobilise significantly elevated support for the management of African protected areas". The support must come from both African governments and the international community. Such support will both enhance the conservation of lions and help to stimulate tourism industry development, economic growth and job creation. Governments should help improve people's ability to raise and maintain livestock and thus ensure they have access to protein without needing to resort to bushmeat. This can be done by providing access to cheap livestock vaccinations and health care to reduce disease, and applying interventions for reducing losses to carnivores.

Cub cuddling and lion walking

The Western public's sentimental love of lions may one day help to ensure their survival; but it also presents conservationists with some tricky ethical dilemmas.

In 2014, the R100 million Lion and Safari Park at Broederstroom in the foothills of the Magaliesberg, north of Johannesburg, was judged Gauteng's biggest tourist attraction. Among its prime drawcards were the lion cubs raised in the park for cuddling by visitors. When the cubs were no longer cuddly, the males were sold on to canned-hunting farms and the females killed for the Far Eastern bone trade. In 2015, CACH persuaded this relatively new park to stop the practice and change its advertising. Soon, the tourist agencies were diverting tourists away from the park, sending them to rival parks that did allow lion cub petting. The drop-off in tourists hit the Lion and Safari Park's business to such a degree it would have gone broke in a matter of months. CACH's director, Linda Park, sympathised with them and agreed to slacken the pressure while seeking an alternative solution; and at least one campaigning body – Citizens

Against Poaching – expressed its "bitter disappointment" at this about-face. Overseas visitors to Africa want to cuddle lion cubs, presumably unaware of their fate. It's a multimillion-rand dilemma.

Merging the parks

Most game reserves occupy land that agriculturally is at best marginal. With the burgeoning of international tourism stimulated by education, books, films and television, this marginal land is gaining in economic importance. However, most national parks are simply not big enough for megafauna to live in dynamic equilibrium. Many are virtually game ranches, and have to be tightly managed. Even Kruger Park with its 20,000 square kilometres – almost comparable to Belgium or Massachusetts – has had serious problems with, for instance, elephant. There was a period in the 1970s when, through overpopulation, elephants trashed large areas, thus reducing the territory's carrying capacity for smaller animals and seriously affecting its biodiversity. Thousands had to be shot, and the meat was sold to the gold-mine workers' hostels.

Several points emerged from the *Beyond Cecil* conference in Entebbe in May 2016 and the WildCru meeting at Oxford. It became clear that as Africa's human population carries on growing exponentially – from 1.2 billion, currently, to the 2.47 billion projected for 2050 – more land is going to be needed for housing and agriculture. Cultivated land in sub-Saharan Africa is expected to increase by 21% and livestock by 73% within this same period. Improved land-use planning and farming in Africa could achieve higher yields on less land, and housing needs to break from the traditional, but unsustainable, low-density wasteful patterns of rural sprawl in order to make more land available for crops.

One delegate said: "Solutions exist and they are not complicated, but will require a global response. Perhaps the single most important step in securing a future for the lion in Africa is mobilising massive support for the continent's vast system of protected areas. If secured, their land area would ensure the long-term survival of the lion and that of many other species. African protected areas incorporate 1.51 million square kilometres of lion range (an area 24% bigger than South Africa's landmass.)

"Reinforcing protected areas ... would require an annual budget of at least $1.25 billion."

This would indeed be the lion's salvation. And it is happening. An Africa-wide trend is afoot towards consolidating and coalescing existing, but scattered, parks and reserves. As I describe in the next chapter, reserves in many parts of Africa have been uniting – even across international borders. For some years, a group of five contiguous countries in Central Africa has been engaged in talks to amalgamate their respective parks into the biggest international park in the world. South Africa's Kruger Park has already taken down several kilometres of its fence with Mozambique's Limpopo National Park, with the option to connect with several more parks in Mozambique and Zimbabwe. Kruger has also begun to absorb privately owned and provincial reserves to its west, right up to the Mpumalanga escarpment.

There's a potential for an international park along the line of the Limpopo River and even further to the west, across Botswana and Namibia – potentially stretching from the Indian Ocean to the Atlantic. Even Tanzania's Selous Game Reserve (which is not a national park, for it allows hunting), can amalgamate with Mozambique's Niassa National Reserve to the south by incorporating the 60-kilometre-wide corridor of land that lies between. The two reserves are each the size of

Switzerland. The inhabitants of the scattered villages in the mainly wild country between them would not need to abandon their lifestyle, for they already live with wild animals; but they would need to share in the tourist income, and clearly perceive the benefits of their new status.

Land use

A major factor in the loss of lion numbers across Africa as a whole has been the change in land use, especially the loss of habitat to agriculture. Lions now occupy only about 8% of their historical range. Converting to agriculture is not always a rational choice. Tanzania, which years ago signed a convention agreeing to cherish the Serengeti as a UNESCO World Heritage Site, was considering growing wheat there – for export. This would have been tantamount to converting one of the most famous pieces of biologically rich East Africa into a monoculture for the sake of selling its produce to another country. It somehow smacks of selling one's own mother.

Agriculture is not the only threat. Another Serengeti project, to build a highway through the reserve, was defeated in court by activists, who in their submission cited a 2012 highway project in Benin where, "within months" of the arrival of a Chinese road crew, two workers had been arrested with lion skins and bones. Apart from their obvious destruction of habitat, such highways also make it easier for poachers to operate.

Reintroducing lions

The story of lions in Zululand is of great relevance for those with hopes of restoring lion populations elsewhere in Africa. When I was first there in 1958, lions had long been extinct. By happenstance, I had chosen a critical time for my visit. I was told, in the strictest confidence by a ranger, that a male lion had wandered in from Mozambique. That lion was to trigger a chain of events that no-one foresaw. Rangers in the various game reserves in Zululand were ecstatic, and put out a not terribly convincing story that it was, in fact, a large hyena. They were hoping the lion would find sanctuary in one of the reserves spread across Zululand. Meanwhile local farmers, equally enthused, had set up 24-hour patrols hoping to shoot it. Gordon Bailey, a senior game ranger and now retired, recently sent me a fascinating account of what happened. It marvellously illustrates how a wild lion population can be restored: "There wasn't a game ranger on the staff in iMfolozi that had any lion experience before the arrival of that first lion in 1958. The reason was that an epidemic of cat flu during the 1930s, and the persistence of local hunters, wiped out the lion population. So when the news broke of a large male lion heading south from Mozambique, the game rangers hoped he would find his new home in iMfolozi.

"The lion's exit was caused by Mozambique hunters who fortunately ceased the hunt when the lion crossed into Zululand. News of the lion's presence spread through the local Zululand community like a veld fire and a surprisingly large number of people started cleaning and oiling their rifles in feverish preparation. The (Natal) Parks Board staff working in the game reserves of Ndumo, Mkhuzi, Hluhluwe and iMfolozi were also keeping a close eye on the newcomer's progress – for different reasons. The (Zulu) game guards employed in the reserves lived in nearby villages and reported anything that indicated the direction he was headed. The phone never stopped ringing in Ian Player's office (the ranger in charge of iMfolozi) as farmers sought information of the lion's whereabouts, and he fed them false leads. The rangers remained on constant alert and, when using the short-wave radio band between the various reserves, they never discussed the lion. The lion eventually made it to the Dukuduku Forest east of Mtubatuba where for three days he was hunted relentlessly by several groups and we thought he would meet his end there.

"You can imagine the excitement when early one morning they got the news that the lion had walked right down the main road of Mtubatuba one night. Two days later he was seen almost on the iMfolozi doorstep.

"Suddenly all news of him died away.

"A week later a game guard based at one of the guard camps in the iMfolozi wilderness area was cycling back into iMfolozi after four days' leave. He was halfway across a dry sandy stream bed when the head of a huge black-maned lion appeared out of the phragmites (reeds) on his right. He promptly fainted. When he came to he jumped up quickly, inspecting his body to make sure nothing of him had been eaten. He grabbed his bike and sped to Ogome outpost to report the incident to (game ranger) Nick Steele. Nick immediately drove to the site and the signs in the sand told the whole story. He saw the impression of where the game guard had lain but what was far more interesting was that, while he was still in a faint, the lion had emerged from the reeds and walked in a complete circle around the body, obviously smelling the man on the ground. The signs on the ground were very clear; the front pug marks closest to where the game guard had lain, because of the weight distribution as the lion stooped to smell the game guard, were the deepest. The lion had travelled over 300 kilometres and much of the route would remain a mystery, but his presence in iMfolozi was the start of a new learning curve for all the game reserve staff.

"The conditions in iMfolozi were decidedly suitable for the new arrival as the antelope populations were at their peak in numbers. Two weeks after his arrival the first of his magnificent roars was heard.

"How thrilling it was to hear him proclaiming ownership to his new territory. His presence was the start of a much needed natural predation game removal system. Before his arrival all game removal was done by rifle. However, his loneliness later began to raise a real concern amongst the game rangers: 'How long would he stay without a mate?'

"At that time Ian Player's famous relocation programme, Operation Rhino, was in full swing and the Kruger National Park was the biggest recipient of the captured rhino. Rhino were taken by truck from iMfolozi in large solidly built wooden crates and after being off-loaded in the national park, the trucks then returned to iMfolozi with the empty crates. It was a complete mystery how it happened, but when one of the crates was offloaded back at iMfolozi, rangers witnessed a magnificent lioness stepping out, followed by three eight-month-old female cubs. She showed no hesitation or nervousness during her exit as most animals would when being reintroduced to a new area. She stepped out with a beautiful confidence, followed by her cubs, and walked directly to the nearest acacia tree and, standing her full length, reached up and ran her extended claws down through the bark of the thick trunk several times. She then lifted her head high, scenting the air flow around her; chose her direction and after several deliberate flicks of her tail walked off with her cubs. Everybody stood rooted for nearly half an hour and finally it came, a low communication call. She did it several times, lapsing into brief silence between the calls, and then it happened: the powerful answering roar of the male. There was triumph clearly written on every face and after cheers and handshakes the watchers departed.

"Conditions at the time could not have been more suitable, normal rainfall had exceeded the annual average, and the iMfolozi /Hluhluwe complex enjoyed some of its best years. During this time we experienced a lion population explosion. Their numbers were growing and territorial areas were being established. Lions were yet to move north into (neighbouring) Hluhluwe when I was called to Hluhluwe's main camp office one day. A tourist, Doug Cole, introduced himself saying that he had seen lion spoor. I drove down there with him. The spoor ... was clearly the front imprint of a male. There were four lions, possibly all males, in the group and they were headed north. On my return I spoke to Nick Steele and we knew we were in for some serious problems if the lions went through the fence in any direction around the reserve. The worst problem would be the loss of any human life. Compensation for the loss of livestock or food crops could always be sorted, but the loss of human life would have a disastrous impact on families and would surely signal the eradication of the whole lion population.

"The good conditions being experienced in the game reserve were also being enjoyed in the different grazing areas of the tribal authorities that surround our boundary. Soon the fragrant scent of the fattening cattle beyond our fences raised the curiosity of our iMfolozi residents and, inevitably, they went through the fence. What a rich protein find: the cattle, not knowing lions, did not run away. What better place to establish new territorial areas where your meal waited for you to help yourself? When the first three lions left the southern boundary we placed a drugged impala carcass a few metres inside the reserve fence at the point they had exited. Luckily they returned that night and fed on the drugged carcass. We tagged them and relocated them almost 50 kilometres from where they had left the reserve. Four days later they went out again. When Nick's report reached head office, the immediate response from the board was that all lions leaving the reserve were to be shot on sight. The lions were magnificent specimens and none of the game rangers enjoyed destroying them, and none of us kept score.

"During my years as the ranger in charge, there was no loss – neither inside nor outside the reserves.

"Since those days at least 200 lions have had to be shot."

Bailey's account of the reintroduction of wild lions into a suitable habitat is just one of many examples of how quickly lions can re-establish themselves. Lions have also been reintroduced into a game park not far from iMfolozi – the recently consolidated iSimangaliso Wetland Park, which includes the St Lucia estuary, Africa's largest estuary. To reduce the breeding rate in the 230-kilometre-long wetland, one horn of the uterus has been removed from each lioness. It is too early to tell how effective this will be.

The Kenyan petting zoo

For the last 40 years overseas donors have poured vast sums into Kenya with the proviso that it bans hunting – even culling. The government-controlled Kenya Wildlife Service (virtually the sole custodian of all Kenya's wildlife) found it could make more money from overseas donations than from safari hunting, and so shaped its policy to satisfy its donors in Europe.

Overnight, lions became vermin in the eyes of Kenyans. Gone were the safaris and their wealthy clients who had paid big money to shoot a lion. Safari operators had employed a lot of people as camp organisers, drivers, skinners, butchers and cooks to keep the big camp pot going. Once the big-spending hunters disappeared, the lions had no value at all to the locals, and were shot, speared and poisoned by cattle farmers. Eco-tourists and photographers might compensate for the loss of hunters, but only in areas where the scenery is attractive. A lot of lion country is fairly mundane and unattractive from the point of view of eco-tourists.

In 2007 the Kenyan land-use economics researcher Mike Norton-Griffiths criticised KWS, as well as Europe's wildlife societies, for supporting unrealistic and ineffective wildlife policies, driven not by science but by the overseas public's love of lions and their interpretation of what lions – and Africa – needed. He said wildlife protectionists (as opposed to conservationists) massively influence wildlife management in Africa, yet are unaware of the needs of rural Africans and are ignorant of the market forces that determine land use and the needs of wildlife. From their homes in Cincinnati, Birmingham or Frankfurt, animal lovers, rather than scientists, are determining wildlife policies in Africa.

This situation struck me forcibly in 2012 when I was invited to Kenya to see its eco-attractions, at a time when Kenya was keen to attract South African tourists. In my week-long visit I was shown only one sizeable reserve – Ol Pejeta – where, to my amazement, the main objective was to show me some chimpanzees in an enclosure. Chimps are not even indigenous to Kenya. They were lolling in the short grass while tourists viewed them from an elevated platform. There was no time for me to see the reserve's interesting variety of antelope or its great birdlife. Instead I was shown a captive, blind black rhino, and invited to feed it. The day before, I was taken on to a raised platform somewhere else so that I could feed a bag of pellets at head height to a giraffe. Certainly, I saw during that week some magnificent lions, leopards and cheetahs – all in cages or pens. Many had pet names and had been reared as orphans.

Every day, I was taken to an animal orphanage, and I began to realise that Kenya perceives that this is what eco-tourists want. And maybe it is what they want. Apparently animal lovers are not offended to see chimps in a paddock in a Kenyan game reserve, and are thrilled to be able to feed a tame rhino or giraffe.

Scenically, the limited area of Kenya that I was shown was mundane – until I got to the Mount Kenya Safari Club. Yet, even there, I was taken to an animal orphanage; or perhaps it was a menagerie. Kenya is becoming an expensive petting zoo.

This can hardly be the future of conservation in Africa.

5 The elephant – down, but not out

I remember a remark made by a girl about
her father, a businessman of narrow
sensibilities, who, casting about for a means
of self-gratification, travelled to Africa and slew
an elephant. Standing there in his new hunting
togs in a vast and hostile silence, staring at the
huge dead bleeding thing that moments before
had borne such life, he was struck for the first
time in his headlong passage through his days
by his own irrelevance. "Even he," his daughter
said, "knew he'd done something stupid".

Peter Matthiessen, *African Silences*

It was a bit of a grey day in Nairobi in July 2016. Even though the national park is well away from the city centre one could still see the smoke to the south, billowing up into the sky. One wonders if the prisoners in the notoriously overcrowded Nairobi jail saw it too, and what thoughts went through their heads.

Most of the city knew what the fires were about. President Uhuru Kenyatta had called in a team of the pyrotechnic specialists who create spectacular fires for Hollywood movies. They had poured hundreds of litres of petrol on to twelve large pyres of carefully stacked elephant tusks. The tusks came from 8,000 elephants killed by poachers, some of whom were now serving long sentences in Nairobi's foetid jail.

For the past week, dozens of workers had been emptying confiscated shipping crates filled with elephant tusks, originally destined for the Far East – 105 tonnes of them. Some tusks were so big it took two men to carry them. On one heap were some beautifully carved ivory statuettes weighing several kilograms.

There was well over a tonne of rhino horns too, from 343 rhinos killed by poachers. And colobus monkey skins, and highly flammable sandalwood, illegally obtained from the now endangered *Santalum paniculatum* tree, for which the perfume manufacturers were prepared to pay wood poachers high prices; and medicinal bark, illegally stripped by *mgangas* (witch doctors) from various increasingly rare trees.

Ceremoniously, in front of diplomats from other elephant-owning states, conservationists, and a silent crowd, Kenyatta put the first pyre to the torch. Soon, all twelve were blazing. Had they reached the black market, the goods would have been worth one-and-a-half times as much as Kenya annually spends on wildlife conservation. Kenyatta told the onlookers that the purpose of the exercise was to put the confiscated goods "beyond economic use". The stockpile was not valuable, he said. It was worthless.

The director of the Kenya Wildlife Service (KWS), General Kitili Mbathi, said: "The only value of ivory is when (it is) on a live elephant."

It was not the first time Kenya had set fire to tonnes of tusks, and probably not the last.

Elephants, survivors of the Pleistocene's megafauna, have been around for 20 million years and have adapted to living in deserts, in canopy jungle, and on mountains; until human hunters arrived, these proboscideans thrived as mastodons and mammoths in Siberia's freezing tundra.

In 2006, Dr Gay Bradshaw, an American ecologist and animal psychologist from Oregon, identified a disturbing new trait among elephants – Indian elephants as well as African. Bradshaw is a double PhD respected for her insights into animal trauma and the field of Human-Wildlife Conflict (HWC) and, in particular, human-elephant conflict. She sparked debate among fellow scientists by identifying post-traumatic stress disorder (PTSD) in elephants. In an article headed *Elephant Breakdown* in the science journal *Nature,* Bradshaw and associates suggested that elephants are displaying increased animosity towards humans.

She wrote, "Everybody pretty much agrees that the relationship between elephants and people has dramatically changed. What we are seeing today is extraordinary. Where for centuries humans and elephants lived in relatively peaceful coexistence, there is now hostility and violence".

Bradshaw said elephants were behaving in a way never before encountered because they are suffering from a form of "chronic stress" brought about by years of poaching, culling and ever-shrinking habitat. "Stress has so disrupted the intricate web of familial and societal relations by which young elephants have traditionally been raised in the wild, and by which established elephant herds are governed, that what we are now witnessing is nothing less than a precipitous collapse of elephant culture".

The research added a new element to the debate about the commercial exploitation of the world's largest land mammal: is the elephant to be looked upon as a resource, like coal or coffee beans? Or is it to be viewed as an extraordinary animal that is part of Africa's unique image – part of the continent's fascination? Does it have a right to exist?

Bradshaw's view was reinforced by Britain's *New Scientist,* which reported in February 2006 that elephants appear to be attacking human settlements in India "as vengeance for years of abuse". The science news journal was reporting on a paper by Joyce Poole, a PhD research director at the Amboseli Research Project in Kenya, who said, "They are certainly intelligent enough to have good enough memories to take revenge." She cited cases where the matriarch of a herd (elephant herds are led by females) had been killed, leaving leadership to inexperienced "teenaged mothers". This, combined with a lack of older bulls, produced a generation of dangerous elephants – "teenaged delinquents".

One can certainly spot the trend in South Africa. In Kruger National Park, bull elephants that are characteristically even-tempered have, without obvious provocation, turned cars over. There have so far been no fatalities in these incidents. However, a German expat neighbour of mine, visiting the Pilanesberg National Park northwest of Johannesburg, left his car and walked into the bush with his five-year-old daughter who probably needed the toilet. They were charged by one of a pair of elephants, which they appear not to have seen until too late. The father threw his daughter under a bush (thus saving her life) and ran in the opposite direction to draw the animal away. A ranger told me, "We found his lungs 100 metres from his body". The man had been tusked, trampled and torn apart. The two elephants then rolled his car over and over into the veld.

In the early days of Pilanesberg National Park – it was farmland when I first visited it in the 1960s, more scenic than productive – a young elephant broke through the fence into dried-out maize lands. A helicopter circled looking for it. One of the observers told me, "I spotted among the sea of brown, dried maize stalks a bright crimson patch at a farm gate and what remained of the farmer's body. The elephant had crushed him against the fence posts and smashed him to pieces".

Pilanesberg's elephants were introduced to the reserve after being captured as orphaned calves after Kruger Park's culling operations. They had known terrible trauma; they had seen their mothers rushing around in blind panic and then dropping as a helicopter clattered above carrying a marksman with a drug gun. The young survivors became undisciplined delinquents and in a couple of years accounted for two more (non-tourist) deaths as well as the deaths of 60 white rhinoceroses. The mayhem stopped only when adult elephants were introduced.

In contrast, wild elephants in habitats undisturbed by hunters frequently display an affinity for humans. Some, brought up or befriended by humans and later returned to the wilds, will many years later recognise them, or the sound of their vehicle, from a distance, and rush up to greet them with the terrifying joyfulness of a 5-tonne puppy. I recall reading of an elephant mother with a chronically sick calf taking it to the elephant orphanage where she'd been raised years before, seeking help.

Few people appreciate how empathetic these generally placid animals are to each other. I am tempted to be even more anthropomorphic and say they behave in a "civilised way". As Rudyard Kipling wrote in his poem *Oonts*, "The elephant's a gentleman". Their social attitudes are uncannily human, and one would have to be quite insensitive not to be touched by some of scenes one sees or hears about. While this chapter was being written, Sharon Pincott's *Elephant Dawn* was published. It's an extraordinary story of how an Australian corporate executive gave up her career to live with a close-knit community of elephants in Zimbabwe and became accepted as one of the family, and how, inevitably, the poachers and hunters – backed by politicians – closed in. And anybody who has read Iain and Oria Douglas-Hamilton's 1975 book, *Among the Elephants*, or, more recently, Lawrence Anthony's unforgettable *The Elephant Whisperer* or Daphne Sheldrick's *Love, Life and Elephants* will surely have been moved by the accounts of the intelligence of these animals and the firm bonds that bind their families and communities. I have witnessed more tenderness and solicitude watching the behaviour of extended families of elephants than among some human families. A lot more.

Graeme Shannon, a Sussex University psychologist working in Kenya, found elephants could distinguish between different languages. If people spoke English, the language of the tourists with their clicking cameras, the elephants were relaxed. If they heard the language of the Maasai whose warriors attack them, they became agitated, yet if that same person switched to Swahili, the language of the urban Kenyan, they calmed down. He tells the story of an incident in an English circus in the early 1900s when an Indian elephant, maddened by something, became uncontrollable and ringside people began to panic. A man stepped out of the audience, walked towards the elephant and spoke to it in Hindi, the language the elephant was familiar with in India. It immediately calmed down. The man (so the story goes) was Rudyard Kipling.

Animal psychologist Karen McComb, also at Sussex and who researched elephant communication, said, "it is the empathy of elephants that stands out, that makes them seem so like humans. My (wholly unscientific) research on elephants squares with the conclusions of Prof. Richard Byrne, of the University of St Andrews, when he wrote: 'What elephants share with humans is that they live in an elaborate and complex network in which support, empathy, and help for others are critical for survival'."

According to the David Sheldrick Wildlife Trust – the trust rescues elephants and rehabilitates them – a live elephant, over its life, generates 76 times more in tourism revenue than it does for its ivory. The group's founder, Daphne Sheldrick, named the Nairobi-based trust after her late husband, popular warden of Tsavo East National Park. Rather pessimistically she believes her great-grandchildren will not witness elephants in the wild.

Of all the megafauna, this pachyderm is the most loved by visitors and tourists to Africa. No matter how many times one sees elephants in the bush, one is always astonished at how silently even a big herd weighing hundreds of tonnes can move on their cushioned feet and disappear, totally, into the bush a mere 50 metres away. One is left wondering whether they were there in the first place. Africa without elephants would have lost its magic and its allure. And, to be materialistic, Africa would have lost an anchor species in its $80 billion tourist industry.

A world without elephants would be a damning indictment of *Homo sapiens,* for it would be our fault entirely.

More and more people are starting to appreciate the importance of biodiversity and the elephant's interesting, complicated and vital ecological role in maintaining that biodiversity. Many people I know admit to feeling a distinct emotional attachment to them.

However, this emotional attachment is not generally felt by rural Africans, who are unable to see any advantage at all in having elephants around them; and it is easy to see why. In *Save Me from the Lion's Mouth* – an examination of Human-Wildlife Conflict (HWC) – I described the trauma of people living in elephant country where crops are devastated, huts demolished and neighbours killed in the growing competition for *lebensraum.*

If elephants are to continue on this Earth, human grievances must be addressed. People who have them as neighbours must derive tangible benefits from the situation – as a matter of urgency. The reality, according to the 2008 Food and Agriculture Organization (FAO) working paper – *Human-Wildlife Conflict in Africa* – prepared by the International

Foundation for the Conservation of Wildlife, is that the rural dwellers' antipathy towards elephants "goes beyond that expressed for any other wildlife". People living in parts of Africa "fear and detest" them. It is a challenge whose seriousness few well-meaning conservationists appreciate.

Kenya's courts were busy. A few weeks after the Nairobi ivory burn, Feisal Mohamed Ali, one of the country's most prolific ivory dealers, was sent to prison for 20 years. He was also fined $200,000 for possessing 413 pieces of ivory valued at over $400,000. In June 2014, two tonnes of ivory allegedly belonging to Ali had been found in a warehouse in Mombasa, Kenya's second-largest city. Ali fled to Tanzania, and Kenya asked Interpol to help. But, as Shakespeare would have put it, Kenya had "scotched the snake, not killed it" – a major part of the prosecution's exhibits, consisting of nine vehicles laden with ivory, disappeared while in the care of the police.

The Kenyan government had previously been remarkably light on sentencing. It was common knowledge that Jomo Kenyatta's first wife, Grace, who died in 2007, was involved in big-time ivory smuggling. In 2015, however, Kenya warned that penalties would become more severe. One magistrate didn't hear: he fined a Chinese man a mere $350 for illegally possessing 400 pieces of ivory, at a time when ivory was fetching nearly $2,500/kilogram on the black market – quite a bargain for the accused. Slowly, however, the message did seem to be reaching the courts. Months later a Chinese woman, arrested boarding a Kenyan Airways flight to Hong Kong carrying 7 kilograms of worked ivory, was sentenced to 31 months in jail. A still more salutary case involved another Chinese national who was ordered to pay the maximum penalty, equivalent to $233,000 (the fine used to be $465) or else go to jail for seven years, for smuggling a single tusk weighing 3.4 kilograms. A spokesman for the Kenya Wildlife Service, Paul Udoto, told the French news agency AFP that it was "a landmark ruling that sets a precedent for those involved in smuggling" and it was "very motivating for our rangers to see poachers lose a lot of money and spend long terms in Kenyan prisons".

In 2015, of 17 smugglers arrested in Kenya, eight were Chinese and six Vietnamese.

For Kenya, protecting wildlife is crucial. Its elephants are vital to its tourist image, and tourism represents 12% of its foreign earnings.

Richard Leakey, palaeo-anthropologist and head of the Kenya Wildlife Service, began his campaign to devalue ivory in the public's mind in 1987, at a time when Kenya was losing 4,000 elephants a year to poachers – more than 10 a day. As chief executive of the KWS, Leakey hit on the innovative and sensational idea of burning Kenya's stockpile of confiscated ivory. A few years later President Daniel Arap Moi, in a big publicity stunt, torched a 12-tonne heap of ivory – the first of the ivory fires. Leakey later claimed, "Within six months of the burn, in 1990, elephant poaching virtually stopped in Kenya and in most African countries because there was no market. The only solution was to kill the market and we did. It was dead for close to 10 years, maybe longer."

His goal was to encourage a total and permanent ban on the trade in elephant ivory; as the rest of this chapter will show, that target remains elusive.

In 1999 South Africa, Zimbabwe, Namibia and Botswana were allowed, amid much controversy, to sell to Japan 60 tonnes of ivory from culled elephants or from elephants found dead in the bush. This was a once-off experimental concession under the CITES convention, which those nations justified on two quite reasonable grounds: southern Africa had so many elephants that they were damaging their own habitat, and the sale raised funds for conservation programmes in Africa. In 2008 another sale was allowed, this time of 107 tonnes of stockpiled government-owned ivory to China and Japan. It sold at $157/kilogram – a massive discount compared to the "normal" black market price which was at least 10 times higher. The sale raised $15 million but it also raised a furore. Richard Leakey believed the sale provided a boon for ivory smugglers by opening an opportunity to launder tonnes of illicit tusks. Events were to prove him right. The sudden rise in demand for ivory and the concomitant renewed slaughter of elephants that followed were, he said, because those sales stimulated the market. Smuggling certainly became easier, helped by rampant corruption – rising, in many countries, right up to ministerial level.

Grace Ge Gabriel, the Asian regional director of the International Fund for Animal Welfare (IFAW), said, "The legal trade clearly removed the stigma attached to buying ivory, thus fuelling demand. This left confused customers, rich criminals and dead elephants. We must learn from the lessons of the past and not repeat the same mistakes. Ivory sales belong in the history books, and any proposals for one-off sales can and must be rejected. If not, we know that elephants will pay the ultimate price."

The Chinese consumers who are driving today's frantic demand for ivory were probably not even aware of Kenya's first ivory bonfire. "They never saw the 1989–1990 elephant crisis," said Leakey in 2016. "So we have to do it again. We want to introduce a sense of embarrassment and shame to the use of (ivory) products for ornaments, for statues or for eating implements – nobody should be using someone else's teeth to enrich themselves".

Leakey's strategy *could* work, but only if it is followed by all the elephant-owning nations. Not everyone agrees that destroying ivory is the best approach. Still, in recent years country after country has been burning piles of illicit tusks, ivory ornaments and jewellery in ostentatious bonfires. In May 2015, Mozambique, having lost half its elephants to poachers in five years, burned its 2.5-tonne stockpile of seized ivory and ivory from natural deaths. It also burned 200 kilograms of rhino horn. In June, America destroyed – by crushing – a tonne of ivory in New York. Hong Kong, a major port of entry for illegal ivory, began in the same year to systematically burn and crush 28 tonnes of ivory. Since 1989, when it became illegal to trade in ivory, 14 countries have destroyed over 130 tonnes. From 2013 to 2016, 11 countries destroyed 80 tonnes.

Even little Belgium burned 1.5 tonnes. China, the world's biggest importer of ivory, somehow found only 1.2 tonnes to burn.

The WWF and the UK Cambridge-based international wildlife monitoring group, TRAFFIC, believe that the destruction of illegal ivory must be backed by rigorous documentation, including an independent audit of the ivory slated for destruction. They say this will reduce the risk that some of it could leak back into the black market. They feel that all countries, even those that have destroyed their current stockpile, should put in place transparent and accountable stock management measures to manage the future ivory stockpiles that will inevitably arise.

WWF also called for "ivory destructions to be backed up with additional law enforcement efforts to combat poaching and trafficking, a stronger judicial process to end impunity for wildlife criminals, and enhanced local stewardship of natural resources".

Botswana

The diplomats who witnessed the 2016 Kenyan burn were also there to attend a summit on future strategy for safeguarding the world's last elephants. However, Botswana, one of Africa's richest nations in terms of wildlife, declined the invitation. Botswana may now also have Africa's largest stock of elephants, since Tanzania has been smuggling its ivory to the Far East. The Botswanan wildlife minister, Tshekedi Khama, felt the public burning of ivory sent a wrong message: "We have told communities living with elephants that there is value in conserving elephants for eco-tourism and emphasising that the value of a live elephant should be upheld at all costs. Burning ivory would demonstrate to the communities that the animal has no value." He appears to have misunderstood the purpose of the demonstration, which was to show that ivory, once detached from the elephant, has no value.

Botswana has, nevertheless, been losing elephants in its remote northern region, where local people – who are said to resent the loss of income from the now banned hunting safaris – helped Angolan and Namibian poachers kill 30 to 50 elephants in 2015. The wildlife veterinarian Clay Wilson, in his 2013 book *Bush Vet*, describes how he vigorously protested the poaching and, for his pains, was arrested and imprisoned without charge in an overcrowded cell under conditions that were quite as appalling as Africa's worst. He realised the poaching was being condoned by people high up in government.

Three years later Tshekedi Khama declared at the Johannesburg CITES conference that all hunting had ended in his country. No more trophies would be allowed out. But as always, there was a gap between the legislative intentions and the reality. Weeks later, Mike Chase of the Great Elephant Census announced at the annual African Indaba in Durban that at least 26 elephants had "recently" been poached in the eastern Linyanti area of Botswana's Chobe enclave where some 150,000 elephants roam between Zimbabwe, Botswana, Namibia and Angola. The elephants had been killed between the Linyanti

Bush Camp, the public camping site, and less than 3 kilometres from the Botswana Defence Force's camp.

In 2015, Angolan poachers in Botswana, in full view of tourists on the Namibian side of the border, opened fire on a herd of 40 elephants, killing four and wounding an unknown number. In 2016, Amos Ramokati, Botswana's regional wildlife officer in Maun, admitted that since the government's 2014 ban on commercial and trophy hunting, there had been an increase in local people assisting poachers. In the past, they had backed efforts to stop poaching. However, after the hunting ban many rural communities lost the substantial income they had been receiving from licensed hunters. Some, like those in the Khwai River area of the Okavango, had been getting an annual income of over $250,000, according to the IUCN's Southern African Sustainable Use Specialist Group.

Tanzania

Kenya's southern neighbour Tanzania, one of Africa's most corrupt countries, years ago descended into industrial-scale poaching. Its government confirmed that in the five years following 2009, Tanzania's population of elephants dropped from 109,051 to 43,330 – a 60% reduction. Allowing for an annual birth rate of 5%, the number of dead must have been over 85,000. The Selous Game Reserve – the world's largest – lost 30,000 elephants out of almost 45,000.

The blasé Minister for Natural Resources and Tourism, Lazaro Nyalandu, said poachers were the "probable" reason for his country's "unimpressive" situation.

John Scanlon, the secretary general of CITES, said: "These figures reinforce our grave concerns about the scale of poaching of elephants in Tanzania for their ivory, and the smuggling routes through Dar es Salaam and neighbouring ports."

Steven Broad, executive director of TRAFFIC, said: "It is incredible that poaching on such an industrial scale has not been identified and addressed before now." He called it "catastrophic". Tanzania is today the largest source of poached ivory.

Symptomatic of Tanzania's self-destructive undermining of its tourist potential is what has happened in the country's 50,000 square kilometre Ruaha-Rungwa ecosystem, which includes the Ruaha National Park. It is one of the most beautiful reserves in Africa, comprising savanna grassland, extensive wetlands, evergreen forest and open woodland. Its more than 570 bird species make it one of the richest birding areas in the world. Ruaha-Rungwa had more than 34,000 elephants in 2009; now there are 8,000. WWF's global species programme director Carlos Drews said the slaughter "clearly points to the involvement of international organised crime, which is compounded by corruption and weak enforcement capacity in Tanzania".

When it comes to the ivory trade, there has been so much shameless dishonesty – mainly in the form of corruption extending high up into government, both in the Far East and in Africa – that it is difficult to get at the truth; but it is clear that China has played a large role in helping Tanzania to destroy its elephant populations. In 2013 the new Chinese President, Xi Jinping, visited Tanzania. Investigators with the Washington-based Environmental Investigation Agency (EIA) claimed that business boomed when Xi's delegation was in the capital city, Dar es Salaam, in March, and the market price doubled. They reported that the Chinese president's entourage bought "thousands of kilos of ivory". Investigators obtained evidence from traders at the city's Mwenge market, which is notorious for ivory trading. "The price was very high because the demand was high," one told undercover investigators. "When the guests come, the whole delegation, that's the time when the business goes up." Another trader said that a 2009 visit to Tanzania by a large delegation led by Hu Jintao, China's president from 2002 to 2012, had created the same phenomenon. He said, "They come to take many things ... then they go direct to the airport, because VIP – no one checks your bags".

The Chinese foreign ministry "strongly dismissed" claims that they had bought so much ivory that prices spiked. Rather quaintly, they said the ministry was "strongly dissatisfied" with the report. "We attach importance to the protection of wild animals like elephants. We have been cooperating with other countries in this area."

However, the new Chinese ambassador to Tanzania in 2014 was honest enough to deplore the role Chinese nationals were playing in Tanzania's illegal wildlife trade, saying "our bad habits have followed us".

More recently, there have been some hopeful signs that Tanzania may be adopting a tougher attitude to smugglers.

In November 2013, three Chinese nationals were arrested at a house in a suburb of the port city of Dar es Salaam, with 706 tusks. The following month, another Chinese was detained while attempting to deliver 81 elephant tusks to two officers from a Chinese naval task force on an official visit to the port. The EIA said that the scale of poaching highlighted the under-funding of the government's wildlife division, whose funding fell from $2.8 million for 2005 to $0.8 million in 2009.

In 2015, Tanzania, perhaps at last embarrassed at being exposed as being almost hopelessly corrupt, announced that its police, in collaboration with Interpol, had seized 1.2 tonnes of ivory and arrested nine suspects in connection with the haul. Criminal Investigation chief Diwani Athumani told the Chinese state news agency Xinhua that another 256 suspects were linked to the crime. What came of it all is unclear, but it seemed that Tanzania was shifting its position. Until 2015 poachers' sentences had been about on a par with traffic fines.

In 2016, Lazaro Nyalandu, Tanzania's Natural Resources and Tourism Minister and the very man who, two years before, had suddenly wondered if poaching had anything to do with the disappearance of 85,000 elephants, announced that 1,082 suspected poachers had been arrested in an "intensified war on poaching". Among those arrested by Tanzania's Anti-Poaching National Task Force was Boniface Mathew Malyango, known as the "King of Ivory" and also as "Shetani Hana Huruma" ("Pitiless Devil"). He was arrested for the illegal possession of 118 pieces of elephant tusks worth about $1 million, "the property of the government". Malyango was described as "the leading trafficker of elephant tusks, running his operations throughout the country." His arrest followed a Zürich customs official's find of 260 kilograms of ivory in eight suitcases dispatched from Dar es Salaam and bound for Beijing. The suitcases also contained lion fangs and claws. In March 2017 Malyango received a 12-year sentence.

That same year, Yang Fenglan (66), a prominent and extremely wealthy Tanzanian businesswoman (owner of a popular restaurant in Mombasa and secretary-general of the Tanzania-China Africa Business Council) was also arrested. She was known as the "Queen of Ivory", the most notorious trafficker in East Africa, who had shipped raw and carved ivory to China over a 10-year period. Many of her suppliers, like Malyango, were also arrested. Yang was charged with smuggling at least 706 elephant tusks worth about $2.5 million. She was lucky enough to get a light sentence – two years' imprisonment – though it is said that two years in a Tanzanian jail is equivalent to a life sentence anywhere else.

In March 2016, two more Chinese nationals were each sentenced to 35 years. They had been arrested in Dar es Salaam in 2013 with hundreds of pieces of elephant tusks and had been in custody for nearly three years.

Tanzania's president, John Magufuli, pledged to root out poaching as part of a wider war on corruption.

Angola

The Angolan civil war, which began in 1975, led to a slaughter of elephants in the south of the country. South Africa's apartheid army, among others, gunned them down and used their ivory to help fund Jonas Savimbi's rebels. The cynicism of it all was illustrated by a gift Savimbi presented to his ally P. W. Botha, the last South African president to commit himself to apartheid: a full-scale Kalashnikov assault rifle made entirely from ivory.

In recent years, the population has started to recover as "refugee" elephants return from Botswana, where they'd found sanctuary.

Despite all the gloomy news about poaching, the overall picture in Africa is that the tables are turning on the poachers. But much remains to be done. As the Environmental Investigation Agency (EIA)'s executive director, Mary Rice, has said, "The ivory trade must be disrupted at all levels of criminality, the entire prosecution chain needs to be systemically restructured, corruption rooted out and all stakeholders, including communities exploited by the criminal syndicates and those on the frontlines of enforcement, given unequivocal support."

The China syndrome

A common thread in all the depredations of Africa by poachers has been the pervasive and baneful influence of China, which has hitherto offered by far the world's richest market for ivory as well as other animal parts.

China's fascination with ivory carvings, some of exquisite design and great value, goes back centuries. The nation's rapidly growing economy and expanding wealthy class enabled more and more people to afford ivory objets d'art and novelties such as paper knives, signature stamps, combs, toothpicks and chopsticks.

Curiously, in the 1980s China officially supported the ban on ivory trading. Rachael Bale of the National Geographic Special Investigations Unit, which focuses on wildlife crime, explained the situation:

"In 1989, the Convention on International Trade in Endangered Species of Wild Flora and Fauna (CITES), the international body that sets wildlife trade policy, banned the global ivory trade. And when an experiment allowed Japan to buy 55 tonnes of ivory legally in 1999, the resulting rise in smuggling caused China to deem the Japan experiment a failure.

"But just a few years later, China began lobbying to be allowed to do the same – to buy a limited amount of ivory to sell domestically, in a tightly controlled market. China lobbied hard, and in 2008, CITES granted its request.

"That year, China legally bought 73 tonnes of ivory from Africa. About that time, it also built the world's largest ivory-carving factory and began opening shops to sell ivory. *National Geographic* went inside some of China's carving factories in 2012 and revealed how China's actions were promoting the legal and illegal ivory trade. Instead of keeping prices for ivory low, the government raised them, making ivory more profitable to poachers.

"China's internal ivory control systems have failed. While 79% of Chinese people surveyed by National Geographic Society and GlobeScan (a public opinion research consultancy) said they'd support a total ban on ivory, the survey also found that 36% of those surveyed in China wanted to buy ivory and could afford it, while another 20% wanted to buy it but couldn't afford it."

After 2010 the Chinese market for ivory grew enormously, along with its demand for rhino horn, as we shall see in the next chapter. Paradoxically, ivory's high price, and the prestige associated with owning this luxury item, was a major contributor to the near-frantic demand.

In May 2016, the WWF and TRAFFIC issued a joint briefing after carrying out a survey of ivory sales in China:

"We believe that an ivory trade ban in China is feasible .... Such an ambitious and achievable act could garner positive exposure for China's responsible action on a critical wildlife conservation issue and become a positive influence on other countries' efforts to tackle the illicit ivory trade. WWF and TRAFFIC would support an ivory trade ban by the Chinese government and stand ready to assist in its implementation and help evaluate future impacts of such a ban in China and around the world."

The briefing, which, in places, is a mixture of the patronising, the cajoling and the prescriptive, says that over the years CITES has consistently identified China as the leading recipient of illicit ivory. It notes that the head of China's State Forestry Administration announced in 2015, "We will strictly control ivory processing and trade until the commercial processing and sale of ivory and its products are eventually halted".

"In September 2015," said the briefing, "during a State visit to the USA, Chinese President Xi Jinping and US President Barack Obama jointly committed to enact nearly complete bans on ivory import and export, including significant and timely restrictions on the import of ivory as hunting trophies, and to take significant and timely steps to halt the domestic commercial trade of ivory".

WWF and TRAFFIC conducted surveys of the legal and illegal ivory markets in 10 Chinese cities, as well as online markets for illicit ivory. They visited 56 certified retail outlets, and collected data from 46. Thirteen were "potentially involved in laundering illegal ivory".

The survey found there are 34 designated factories and 130 retail outlets in China that are licensed to manufacture and trade in ivory. These licenses are renewed every two years. Collectively, they were all due to expire after 31 December 2016.

At least the Chinese Auction Association had issued an auction ban on ivory in December 2011, prohibiting the sale of contemporary ivory. Only ivory products deemed to be pre-1949 "cultural relics" by authorities were allowed to be auctioned.

The WWF and TRAFFIC surveyed markets thought to be selling illegal ivory in five cities (Beijing, Shanghai, Guangzhou, Tianjin and Xiamen) and found 189 outlets engaged in illegal ivory trade – all of them, technically, government-controlled. Small manufactured items accounted for nearly all the items on sale – accessories like bracelets, bangles, pendants, amulets, etc.

Between January and June 2016, TRAFFIC monitored 31 websites and found 5,543 advertisements of nine endangered species available for sale. Three-quarters were ivory. "Because law enforcement agencies, website operators and NGOs conduct regular monitoring, the online illegal ivory trade has remained at lower levels since the second half of 2013. Nevertheless, nearly 700 newly posted ivory advertisements can still be found on the Internet every month".

TRAFFIC's data showed that since 2011, the average price of ivory by weight had remained at US$4,500/kilogram.

It reported that "although the number of displayed items per outlet has decreased compared to survey data from five years ago, the fact that these outlets continue sell ivory is a cause for concern. Ivory trade is flourishing on harder-to-monitor social media platforms, and TRAFFIC foresees the social media as the next major battleground in the fight against ivory trafficking and illegal wildlife trade in general. As far as traders are concerned, transactions made via the social media carry less risk of being caught."

Although the Chinese government administers the legal ivory market, the surveys found 28.3% of retail outlets were suspected to be involved in laundering illegal ivory. Distinguishing legally from illegally sourced ivory products "gives rise to a challenging 'grey area', not only for China's law enforcement officials, but also consumers who wish to remain law-abiding citizens". In reality, according to the briefing, "the Chinese public remains confused regarding the legal nature of ivory trade," with many believing that ivory can be traded freely … "The prevalence of ill-informed consumers and crafty traders presents a worrying combination and obvious challenges to law enforcement". What was most encouraging was that the WWF/TRAFFIC survey showed 79% of respondents in China would support a ban on all buying and selling of ivory in their country.

The briefing estimated that fewer than 3,000 livelihoods would be affected by the ban. The survey found that nearly half of the retail outlets surveyed, and nearly all 34 factories, had already begun to diversify their businesses. For example, at least 19 factories use other materials for sculpting such as mammoth ivory, jade, wood, and bone.

The briefing adds, hopefully, "If the State Council of China were to issue an ivory trade ban, such action would be widely acclaimed and put China in an elevated global leadership position on a vital conservation issue".

The briefing said that the announcement to commit to a ban in ivory trading by China and the USA in September 2015 represented an important global policy commitment, "and its effects have been seen beyond their borders garnering positive feedback from the international community ... 25 African elephant range states announced their support for 'all proposals and actions at international and national levels to close domestic ivory markets worldwide'."

Two months later, Hong Kong's territorial government announced it would end its ivory trade by 2021. This, it said, was to give traders five years to liquidate their stocks. It had earlier ostentatiously begun a months-long process of systematically burning and crushing 28 tonnes of illegal ivory confiscated since 2001. This quantity would have cost the lives of 7,000 to 8,000 elephants.

Singapore also stated its intention to ban ivory trading.

Then came the best news of all: the Chinese state news agency, Xinhua, reported that China "will gradually stop the processing and sales of ivories (sic) for commercial purposes by the end of 2017". Xinhua said the complete ban would affect "34 processing enterprises and 143 designated trading venues, with dozens to be closed by the end of March 2017".

Coming from the world's biggest buyer of ivory – 70% of Africa's illegal ivory finds its way to China – this was momentous news. As Elly Pepper at the New York-based Natural Resources Defense Council put it: "It's a game-changer. It could be the turning point that brings elephants back from the brink of extinction."

Aili Kang, Chinese executive director of the Wildlife Conservation Society in Asia, enthused:

"This is great news that will shut down the world's largest market for elephant ivory. I am very proud of my country for showing this leadership that will help ensure that elephants have a fighting chance to beat extinction. This is a game-changer for Africa's elephants".

Proud of his country? Proud of what? Proud that China for years had shamelessly allowed its criminals to go to Africa, hire poachers, in many cases arm them with advanced weaponry and infra-red scopes to slaughter tens of thousands of elephants to feed ivory plants that the Chinese government itself had set up? It established the industry in anticipation of obtaining a certain volume of legitimate ivory; but when that volume fell short, it knew full well that the volume coming in was way above what the legitimate market could supply. More than 20,000 elephants were killed for their ivory in 20 years, according to the WWF.

It has been known for years that the only way to stop the slaughter in Africa was to kill the markets in the Far East where, often openly, countries were buying their raw ivory via international crime syndicates. The criminals were bribing African rural dwellers, as well as customs officials and, often, government ministers, who were willing to exterminate their elephant populations if the price was right.

Killing the trade at the destination end was essential. The Chinese government, which created the market and technically owns the ivory factories and retail outlets, in 2015 embarked upon a plan to educate China's growing middle class, which covets ivory carvings as a sign of wealth, about the real price of ivory – the massacre of the elephants.

Speaking in Beijing in 2013, during his first visit there, Kenyan President Uhuru Kenyatta told reporters, "The Chinese government understands that poaching is a problem. The most important thing is that they are not just talking about it but working to solve it".

Kenyatta's office later issued a statement that China had agreed to help improve surveillance around national parks and game reserves, and aid Kenya in adding to the ranks of the current 3,000 wildlife rangers who deal with poachers.

Part of China's campaign to devalue ivory for its citizens was the visit to Kenya of two Chinese stars, and their laudable efforts to tell their tens of million fans back home what was happening to Africa's elephants. They posed next to slaughtered elephants and orphaned calves and made impassioned pleas to their countrymen to stop buying ivory trinkets and figurines. One of them, the actress Li Bingbing, a United Nations Environmental Programme (UNEP) Goodwill Ambassador, "confessed" that she had once bought an ivory bracelet "because I had no idea it had come from a killed elephant". She intimated that a lot of Chinese who value ivory ornaments and jewellery have no idea elephants are being killed to provide it.

"Many in Asia do not realise that by buying ivory they are playing a role in the illegal wildlife trade and its serious consequences. As global citizens, we need to take responsibility by learning more about the potential impacts of our lifestyle choices".

A popular Chinese sporting figure, the 7ft 6in international basketball star Yao Ming – he played for the Houston Rockets as well for China – also visited East Africa. He was sponsored by WildAid, which runs an Asia-wide campaign to educate consumers about the plight of the elephants. Back in China, he described the embarrassment of discovering that China was listed by CITES as a member of the "Gang of Eight" – the countries most complicit in the illicit ivory trade. Of the eight, three are suppliers: Kenya, Uganda and Tanzania; three act as conduits: Malaysia, Vietnam and the Philippines; and two are the major destination countries: Thailand and China.

Japan

Japan, which has been a CITES signatory for 37 years, deserves to be added to that "Gang" of delinquent nations, for it has allowed an illicit ivory market to flourish and has singularly failed to control illegal ivory trading. The Washington-based non-profit Environmental Investigation Agency (EIA) identified four Japanese ivory trading companies that, in 2015, offered to sell elephant tusks to undercover EIA investigators for illegal export to China. The EIA documented Japan's history of broken commitments to effectively prevent poached tusks from being sold domestically or for passing on to China. Allan Thornton, president of EIA, whose 2016 report was released just before CoP17, said "Japan's continued effort to promote the ivory trade is a slap in the face of the 29 African states seeking to end domestic ivory trade to protect their elephants". The four Japanese ivory companies were conducting daily ivory sales to Chinese buyers "and boasted of the vast amounts of ivory being illegally exported to China and Hong Kong". Thirty of the 37 Japanese ivory traders contacted by an undercover agent were willing to engage in illegal activity to buy, sell, or fraudulently register a tusk. Most of Japan's ivory tusk imports were from poached elephants.

Danielle Fest Grabiel, EIA Wildlife senior policy analyst, said, "EIA investigations and research over the past 18 months demonstrate that Japan's ivory control system is plagued by loopholes and undercut by weak legislation to such an extent that no meaningful control exists at even the most basic level".

The Vietnamese connection

With stricter controls on direct wildlife imports into China, Vietnam became the new epicentre of the Asian wildlife trade.

In 2016, apparently feeling a bit of pressure, the government of Vietnam announced it was going to destroy 2 tonnes of ivory and 70 kilograms of horn in some ostentatious burning ceremonies. But it was a meaningless, if not fraudulent exercise. Vietnam's wildlife traffickers, after the show was over, continued to do business as usual.

November 2016 saw a possible watershed in international affairs, initiated by the Wildlife Justice Commission (WJC), an independent organisation that exposes and disrupts global criminal networks. Its team of wildlife crime specialists works to ensure that wildlife criminals are prosecuted by their own national authorities, publicly naming names and providing meticulously researched evidence, sifted by its legal team, to help a nation act against its criminals.

The WJC convenes an Accountability Panel made up of high-level individuals who have no direct affiliation to the Commission; in the Vietnam case these included a former president of the International Criminal Court in The Hague. The panel members, who receive no fees beyond their expenses, are asked to examine a "Map of Facts" with a critical eye and form opinions based solely on the facts that have been presented at the hearing. They then decide, on the weight of the evidence, whether to release the facts to the relevant state authorities and make them available for the world to see. The WJC recommends action, but requires guarantees of witness protection and non-victimisation of whistle-blowers. Their first public hearing put the Socialist Republic of Vietnam in the dock.

The hearing followed a year-long investigation into the town of Nhi Khe, a wildlife trafficking hub where Vietnam was allowing the sale of poached animal parts from around the world, including several tonnes of elephant tusks and rhino horns annually.

The WJC's executive director, Olivia Swaak-Goldman, said in her opening remarks, "Evidence will show the massive scale of illegal and cross-border trade in Nhi Khe (where) traders operate with impunity. These criminal networks abuse legitimate systems: international banking, transport and social networks, for huge profits. Unfortunately, we had little reaction from the Vietnamese authorities other than empty assurances.

"A month ago, our undercover operatives were offered 2 tonnes of ivory by traffickers in Hanoi, and physically saw 880 kilograms. We have provisions in international law and national legal systems to stop wildlife crime."

Investigators observed US$53.1 million worth of wildlife parts being trafficked through criminal networks consisting of 51 individuals. The wildlife parts were from up to 907 elephants, 579 rhinos, 225 tigers and other endangered species including pangolin, bear, hawksbill turtles and helmeted hornbills. WJC found that Nhi Khe has expanded into a transnational trading hub and, thanks to social media platforms such as WeChat and Facebook, it can target Chinese buyers as well as others in Southeast Asia. The investigation also found 17 Chinese bank accounts were being used by traffickers to receive payment from their Chinese buyers.

The most devastating evidence came from the traffickers themselves when they talked, unknowingly and sometimes while being clandestinely filmed, to undercover investigators. Pauline Verheij, senior legal investigator with WJC, said investigators visited 20 shops on their first undercover visit in Nhi Khe and identified five major premises for further investigation. "We chose to focus on bigger premises due to the limited time one can remain undercover without arousing suspicion."

A Chinese buyer explained that the Chinese were coming to Vietnam "because controls are very strict in China". She said that she could deliver "anything" to her customers in China and described how to cross the river – the Chinese border – illegally.

The WJC panel's closing declaration read: "Despite the overwhelming body of evidence, prepared by former law enforcement professionals for Vietnamese law enforcement authorities, and extensive diplomatic outreach and engagement of international stakeholders, the Vietnamese government has failed to take decisive action to close down this criminal network."

China accepted the WJC's case file (which was shared with them due to the transnational aspect of the trade) and "began a preliminary investigation". The Vietnamese authorities said nothing.

The WJC has 10 other investigations in play, and considers case proposals from all countries.

The elephant – friend and foe

There's a certain irony in the evolution of elephant tusks. They are, in fact, giant canine teeth. They can grow up to 3 metres long, and a single tusk has weighed over 90 kilograms in a couple of extreme cases. The irony is that tusks evolved over millions of years for many purposes, including defence – only to prove, eventually, a fatal attraction. In the 1970s the average weight of a tusk coming on to the market was about 10 kilograms; by 1990 it was just over 3 kilograms. This indicates that even in those decades poachers were killing any animal, no matter how young, as long as it displayed even a little ivory. After 2010, ivory prices tripled from $750/kilogram to well over $2,000, so that even the newly erupted, 5-kilogram tusk of a juvenile would fetch many thousands of dollars.

According to the Ivory Education Institute in California, ivory carvers regard African ivory as superior to the Asian variety, which discolours more easily and whose grain does not polish as well.

Counting elephants

Days before the 2016 CITES conference (CoP17) in Johannesburg, the IUCN released the most comprehensive survey to date on Africa's elephants. Its *African Elephant Status Report* revealed that in the decade up to 2015, the elephant population declined by 25% across the 38 African countries that have them. Between 93,000 and 111,000 elephants were slaughtered. Poaching was the main cause, but habitat loss was also a factor.

It was found Africa was down to its last 415,000 elephants – nearly 100,000 fewer than 10 years before. (Try to imagine 100,000 elephants.) The new count included 18,000 individuals from previously uncounted populations; hence the report's estimate that the total decline may be as high as 111,000.

Yet the picture regarding the elephants' chances of surviving is nowhere near as gloomy as the figures suggest. According to the report, the census excluded an additional 117,000 to 135,000 elephants that could be living in areas currently not systematically surveyed.

Another count was the Great Elephant Census of 2014– 2016, an aerial survey covering 18 countries across East, Central and West Africa. This $7 million census was funded by Paul Allen, philanthropist and co-founder of Microsoft. It discovered, in a range of hills in a remote region of southern Ethiopia, 3,000 elephants "unknown to anybody".

The combined surveys confirmed that the surge in poaching that began around 2006 and that was, and still is, masterminded almost entirely by criminal syndicates from the Far East, is the main cause for the decline in populations. Habitat loss is adding to the pressure on the persecuted herds.

Judging by these figures, the elephant population for the whole of Africa probably stands at over 500,000. Though the different concentrations are scattered, and some particularly isolated populations are very vulnerable, the numbers are such that the recovery of Africa's elephants north of the Zambezi is certainly possible and even probable, and those south of the Zambezi, where most elephants live, are holding out despite the sudden surge in poaching in the last few years. Indeed, in some parts of southern Africa, the problem for elephants is not extinction but overpopulation.

It is worth bearing in mind that, just over a century ago, uncontrolled hunting had reduced the elephant population in what is now Kruger National Park to about 40 individuals. Today the South African National Parks say there are 16,000 – despite the thousands that have been culled and poached over the years.

The IUCN *African Elephant Status Report*, based on information gathered by its African Elephant Specialist Group's network of experts and observers, said that southern Africa has over 70% of Africa's savanna (bush) elephants, with almost 300,000 animals. East Africa holds about 86,000 (20%) and Central Africa about 24,000 (6%). West Africa continues to hold the smallest population: about 11,000 (less than 3%).

East Africa – the region the IUCN found most affected by poaching – had, according to the report, experienced a reduction of almost 50% in its elephant population in 25 years. On the other hand, since 2006, elephant numbers had stabilised or increased in three East African countries (Uganda, Kenya, and Rwanda), and range expansion was reported in Kenya.

The forest elephant

Since the 1900s, Central Africa's forest elephant population has been substantially affected by poaching. *Loxodonta cyclotis* is a smaller, more slender species of elephant with thinner and distinctly down-pointing tusks compared to the more common bush elephant *(L. africana)* with its sometimes huge, outward-pointing tusks.

The Democratic Republic of the Congo used to possess one of the most significant forest elephant populations in Africa, but it is now "reduced to tiny remnants" according the IUCN. Gabon and Congo now hold Africa's most important forest elephant populations, but both have been affected by heavy poaching. In Cameroon, both the forest and savanna species have been heavily poached. The savanna elephants in Chad have taken heavy losses and those in the Central African Republic have almost completely disappeared.

According to the WWF there are only about 100,000 forest elephants left, mostly living in the dense forests of Gabon. Logging, ivory poaching and bushmeat hunting have accounted for the deaths of thousands of elephants every year.

Writing of African elephants in general, in June 2016, Achim Steiner, Executive Director of the United Nations Environmental Programme (UNEP), in a report titled *Elephants in the Dust,* underlined the seriousness of the situation regarding "mass elephant killings":

"Results from monitoring and systematic surveys conducted under the UNEP-hosted CITES treaty reveal that poaching levels have tripled in recent years, with several elephants killed every single hour of the day. In Central and West Africa, the elephant may soon disappear from whole areas unless urgent action is taken. Organised syndicates ship several tonnes of ivory at a time to markets in Asia, and hundreds of elephants are killed for every container sent. Indeed, this report documents nearly a tripling in the number of large-scale ivory seizures by customs authorities, revealing the scale and heavy involvement of international criminal networks that must be addressed."

The report said what was needed was not just improved law enforcement methods, but international collaboration with the United Nations Office for Drugs and Crime as well as the World Customs Organization and Interpol. It noted that the existence of large elephant populations in southern Africa demonstrated that "both elephants and their habitats can not only be well managed, but, coupled with tourism, can also become a source of income."

The report said West Africa's bush elephant herds were mostly small, fragmented and isolated, with 12 populations reported as "lost" since 2006 in Côte d'Ivoire (formerly the Ivory Coast), Ghana, Guinea-Bissau, Sierra Leone, Togo, Guinea and Nigeria. West Africa in general has suffered appalling losses, in particularly violent and perhaps vengeful poaching incidents. In 2011, according to the World Wildlife Fund, dozens of heavily armed men on horseback butchered hundreds of elephants in Cameroon, removing the tusks of some. A year later at least 86 elephants were killed en masse by raiders in next-door Chad, including 33 pregnant females and 15 calves. Reports spoke of between 300 and 600 killed; whatever the true figure, it was a bitter blow for a country that had only an estimated 1,000 elephants, practically all of them in the Bouba Ndjida National Park. Both raids involved poachers with automatic weapons carrying out coordinated attacks. The WWF said the poachers spoke Arabic, suggesting that the same group might have been involved in both incidents. There are suspicions that the ivory was to finance Islamic extremists. The Washington-based Environmental Investigation Agency claimed that in recent years Al-Shabaab received a large amount of money through ivory and rhino horn smuggling.

When condemning poachers and jailing a token few, one must bear in mind where the top criminals sit. They are never touched. Clearly the governments of Vietnam, China, Thailand and Japan must not only share but also accept the blame for the rape of Africa. Vietnam, in particular, is shielding its crooks, and might need international sanctions before it relents and purges its government departments of accomplices. All these countries are signatories of CITES and all pretend to adhere to its rules, yet for years they have knowingly and shamelessly allowed an almost unfettered trade in Africa's wildlife.

The African angle

The temptation to poach, for a rural African, is understandable: just one tusk may net a poacher enough money to last him years, or send his children to school – though he may also have to share the loot with the regional chief, the police, corrupt game rangers and government officials. Ivory poachers are looked upon with enormous admiration by many communities.

Lawrence Munro from African Parks – he was Field Operations Manager in Malawi – told the WJC hearing at The Hague: "There is no peace in the Parks. Rangers battle with poachers. It's taking its toll on rangers ... Rangers live in the battlefield – unlike war where you are pulled out periodically."

He added that "'Militarisation' is a problematic term in relation to rangers. It denotes exactly what they are not ... Rangers need politicians to step in and tackle the transnational roots of wildlife crime and poaching".

But "battlefield" is an appropriate term for the situation in the African parks. It was said at the Johannesburg CITES conference that 1,000 game rangers and anti-poaching personnel had lost their lives in the 10 years up to 2015. One victim was Roger Gower, a helicopter pilot, who was shot as he circled over poachers in Tanzania in February 2016. He managed to land in the Maswa Game Reserve, near Serengeti National Park, before dying.

The number of poachers killed would be impossible to guess, because many are shot on the spot and left to the hyenas.

Technology may soon be catching up with the poachers. Drones are now being used to spy on poaching parties. Marc Goss, who is managing an anti-poaching project involving drones in Maasai Mara National Reserve, believes a drone can do the work of 50 rangers. He operates a drone from a hand-held iPad to find and follow poachers until security forces can home in on them. The drone can even photograph the poachers for evidence. Unlike helicopters, drones are not easily heard or detected and can operate at night, using heat sensors to detect poachers and pinpoint recently killed, still-warm elephant carcasses. Goss found that drones can also be used to shepherd elephants away from danger zones by using pepper spray; even a drone's buzzing sound is often enough to drive elephants away, because they believe the sound comes from bee swarms, which they fear.

The population paradox

The dichotomy – between the band of countries across the middle of Africa, with their scattered and heavily poached elephant herds, and the nations of southern Africa, with their relatively huge herds and more efficient governments – has, to a degree, polarised conservationists. Elephants across the middle of the continent are indeed vulnerable; but in the south there are too many of them.

The Conservation Action Trust says: "Although elephant populations may at present be declining in parts of their range, major populations in eastern and southern Africa, accounting for over two-thirds of all known elephants on the continent, have been surveyed, and are currently increasing at an average annual rate of 4.0%." Yet, despite the difference in elephant numbers between the two regions, all elephants have been classified as "vulnerable", whether in the overpopulated south or the ravaged north. Between 1996 and 2004 all were classed as "endangered", which many in southern Africa considered unjustified.

Wherever elephants are secure they tend to overwhelm their resources. Ivo Vegter of the South African online news journal *Daily Maverick* wrote a May 2016 article titled *How endangered species destroy the environment*:

"Whenever a reserve finds it has too many elephants, the truth is that it has too many fences. Elephants are natural migrants. For millions of years, when conditions became unfavourable they moved. When they can't, they hammer the environment.

"It's a problem in North West Province's exclusive 750 square kilometre Madikwe Game Reserve (on Botswana's south-eastern border). Its herd has recently swelled to over 1,200 at a time of severe drought and the vegetation is in trouble."

Madikwe, a relatively small, semi-arid reserve, suffers from the malady afflicting nearly all southern Africa's reserves that have elephants: overpopulation. Vegter quotes the province's head of Ecological Services, Pieter Nel, as saying, "It's not yet at the stage where we need to start thinking about something drastic, like culling". Yet it clearly is. In the same breath, Nel admits: "… but we could definitely do with fewer elephants". Wildlife managers are reluctant to talk about culling because they want to avoid the public's wrath. They will talk of "trans-locating" – exporting animals to other reserves. But within southern Africa, translocation has become impracticable. The reserves are "full". Kruger Park is critically overstocked and so are the parks in its northern neighbour, Zimbabwe.

Translocating is not just expensive and impracticable; it is highly disturbing for the peculiar and complex social structure of elephant populations. It is quite as disruptive to elephant society as it would be for humans. And it does not always work. Alan Calenborne, one of the owners of Mziki Game Reserve, told me how, a few years ago, the reserve was offered, free, apart from transport costs, a small herd from a reserve some distance to the north. The offer was accepted, and the elephants were set free in Mziki. Within hours the herd barged through the "elephant-proof" fence and headed for home. The National Parks capture team had, inadvertently, separated one of the cows from her calf. The animals had to be rounded up, darted, and returned to whence they had come. No wonder elephants, facing such trauma, are becoming confused and aggressive. The peripatetic elephants, like the 250 elephants of the smaller (500 square kilometres) Pilanesberg National Park, originally came from Kruger Park, survivors of Kruger's early culling programmes. Many, like Pilanesberg's first elephants, were orphans; they'd never known discipline from adults. Lacking parental control, they turned out to be dangerously delinquent.

About this time Kruger Park began capture-drugging entire elephant families from its elephant-stressed areas and, in some expensive operations, moved them into the adjacent Parque Nacional do Limpopo in Mozambique, which was pretty well "poached out". Many of them soon trooped home. They might have been driven out by poaching activity, for not long afterwards, in May 2015, the US-based Wildlife Conservation Society said poachers had killed nearly half of Mozambique's elephants in the past five years – its 20,000 elephants had been reduced to an estimated 10,300.

As Vegter put it, the standard solution for overpopulation "was to cull or translocate, but the first has become socially unacceptable and the second hugely expensive". To be realistic, the authorities will have to embrace the former. No matter how large future reserves may become, fencing will be necessary and, with no natural constraints on population growth, the elephants will eventually outgrow the space. Some years ago, reluctance to cull along the Chobe River led to the elephants eventually demolishing the once dense riverine forest, which used to provide habitat for black rhino, bushpig, kudu, duiker, leopard and so on. When I last saw it there were just a few stumps of trees, bare sand, and massive erosion.

Vegter quotes Marion Garai, chairman of the South African Elephant Specialist Advisory Group, explaining how the problem could be mitigated by corridors between reserves, such as could exist between Madikwe and, say, smaller reserves such as Mziki and Pilanesberg. Garai said, "Corridors have huge benefits because wildlife can move to different vegetation areas. They can open summer/winter areas and relieve over-grazed vegetation and allow it to recover – the natural pattern for elephants."

Ron Thompson, a South African game ranger, hunter and national park manager with 57 years' experience, was a big voice at the Johannesburg CoP17 conference. He has worked in or managed major national parks throughout southern Africa. He lobbied hard – and unsuccessfully – for reopening the ivory trade. He is the archetypal big-game hunter, and with undisguised pride says he has shot 5,000 elephants (mostly necessary culling work); 800 buffalo (again, a lot on control or for staff meat rations); "fifty or sixty" lions; "thirty or forty" leopards; 140 black rhinos and 20 white rhinos. He pointed out that conservation is not just preservation. By its very definition, it is the wise use of natural resources in a sustainable manner.

His main point in advocating the reopening of the ivory trade is that while elephants are indeed in a parlous situation in Central and East Africa, it is quite the opposite in the southern third of the continent, where there is a growing need to control the numbers. He said, "For this reason alone, the idea of classifying all elephants as "vulnerable" is nonsensical. Different populations might be in danger, stable, or thriving, but to apply the same management criteria and practices to the entire species is not useful".

His elephant figures for the second half of the 20th century are as good as anybody's, considering there were no really comprehensive, scientifically accurate counts until at least the 1980s. Even then, and even much later, censuses were not terribly reliable. Thompson says that in Chobe National Park (in northern Botswana) the elephant population was around 7,500 in 1960. By 1990 there were 54,500 animals (a Botswana government figure). By 2013, there were 207,000 – again according to official figures. That's a doubling of the population every 11 years. He said, "So much for the IUCN's estimate of elephant population growth being 4% per annum or a doubling every 18 years". But the wild upswing in numbers was not due to elephant fecundity alone – it was also due to migration. Annually, tens of thousands of elephants move like a great grey tide across the borders of Namibia, Botswana and Zimbabwe.

Thompson reminded the CITES delegates of the experience in the Gonarezhou National Park on Zimbabwe's border with Mozambique. A cull in 1971/2 took out 2,500 of the park's 5,000 elephants. By 1982 the population was back at 5,000. It was again halved to 2,500. Apart from the damage to the emotional wellbeing of the poor elephants, the damage to the veld was colossal. Nevertheless, the present population is about 11,000 animals, according to Thompson. He said most of southern Africa's reserves have more than their carrying capacity.

In Kruger Park, regular culling since the 1960s kept the elephant population at a level of 7,000, which Thompson says is probably higher than its carrying capacity, which he judged by monitoring the damage to large trees. In the 1950s, a lot of Kruger supported a variety of large trees with plenty of spacing and grazing among them. The huge old mopane trees around Letaba have long been reduced by elephants to shoulder-high scrub. There are very few animals and minimal biodiversity. I recall South Africa's last tall ilala palm tree forest; I suppose it was more of a stand. There were perhaps 100 or so trees outside Letaba Camp. The ilala produces bunches of big shiny brown nuts whose edible kernels – "vegetable ivory" – can become hard enough to make buttons. Its seeds germinate only after passing through an elephant's gut. In the 1960s I was invited to join a group of dendrologists to see what could be done to protect the trees. During the night elephants could be heard crashing about. Next day the country's last ilala forest had been flattened.

Thompson said that around 1960 the tall-tree count around Satara in central Kruger Park was 13 canopy trees a hectare. By 1965 the tree count was nine per hectare. Kruger was culling at the time. A decade later the tree count was three per hectare. By 1981 it was a mere 1.5 canopy trees per hectare. By the millennium, 95% of the tall trees were gone.

Thompson argued that if half of Kruger's elephants had been culled, the damage could have been avoided. The park had not culled elephants for 22 years and there are now 16,000. He says sustainable conservation policies surely ought to be aimed at preserving ecological diversity and processes, "rather than merely increasing the population of a handful of iconic species".

The oversupply of elephants in southern Africa has re-kindled the debates about ivory stockpiles and hunting. At CoP17, the situation encouraged the hunting lobby to seek permission to utilise elephants for hunting; whatever one's stand is on hunting, their arguments were cogent and logical.

Namibia, which has one of the most efficient game management policies in Africa and a reputation for integrity, pleaded for southern Africa's elephants to be moved to Appendix II, arguing that its ivory stockpiles could raise $100 million, which would go back into conservation and water supply in this arid nation.

The pro-ivory sales lobby had originally comprised South Africa, Botswana (which has by far the largest number of elephants of any country in Africa), Zimbabwe, Namibia and Zambia. However, at the conference it became clear that Botswana had changed its position.

Tshekedi Khama, Botswana's Minister of Environment, Wildlife and Tourism, said "the carcasses of too many dead elephants are left to rot by ivory poachers, who smuggle their tusks through global crime syndicates to foreign markets ... The struggle for their protection extends beyond eastern and central Africa ... There is concerning evidence that elephant poaching is moving south. The sophisticated criminal networks that run this trade are fluid, operating over several regions in the continent. Therefore, no population should be considered secure."

This meant that although Botswana had previously supported the limited, legal ivory sales from countries that manage their elephant herds sustainably, "we now recognise we can no longer support these sales, and cannot deal with this issue in a vacuum."

Botswana had recognised that elephants are worth more alive than dead: "In the duration of an elephant's life, it will contribute up to $1.5 million (R14 million) in tourism – that's 16 times the value of what the ivory is."

But the debate at CoP17 conference clearly swung away from the value of ivory – it was about the value of elephants. The pro-hunting/ivory sales delegates failed to convince CITES that elephants should be moved to Appendix II, allowing the ivory trade to resume. The majority of delegates believed that allowing one part of Africa to sell ivory was impracticable because the criminals would launder illicit ivory along whatever channels were opened. So CITES' CoP17, amid applause, overwhelmingly voted for elephants to remain totally protected on "Appendix 1" where they have been since 1989.

Merging the parks

Throughout Africa there are plans in various stages of development to amalgamate near-neighbour reserves, or to link reserves by using corridors. The trend is the result of the steady increase in global tourism – particularly eco-tourism – and to make it easier for the animals and plants in protected areas (PAs) to reach a self-sustaining state of dynamic equilibrium. The smaller the reserve, the more the need to intervene. The trend towards amalgamation has the potential to greatly increase available habitat for elephants.

A group of five Central African states – of the 38 African states with elephants – announced in 2006 they were keen to link their national parks and reserves. In December the tourist ministers of Botswana, Zambia, Zimbabwe, Namibia and Angola – all with borders on the Zambezi River – signed a Memorandum of Understanding to create the world's largest international game park. A feasibility study undertaken by the Peace Parks Foundation and the Development Bank of Southern Africa forecast that this transfrontier park could attract as many as 8 million tourists annually as well as create employment for thousands of people and stimulate socio-economic development across the region. The project, the Kavango-Zambezi Transfrontier Conservation Area (now being called the Kaza Park), will incorporate 280,000 square kilometres of contiguous elephant country in an area as big as Holland, Belgium, Denmark, Austria and Portugal combined, and will stretch across Africa from Angola and Namibia to the Mozambique border. It incorporates 14 already proclaimed national parks, including such charismatic reserves as the Moremi in the Okavango Delta, Chobe National Park, the salt pans of the Kalahari, Zimbabwe's Hwange National Park, Lake Kariba, the Sioma Ngwezi National Park and the Kafue in Zambia. Victoria Falls forms the hub. The idea is that elephants and wildlife in general will be able to roam freely and, one day, so will tourists, using special all-areas visas.

There is another, already progressing, transfrontier park of enormous size south of the Limpopo. Technically it is more of an international conservancy, as it could potentially incorporate private reserves, which might have other functions and attractions apart from simply protecting wildlife – hunting, for example, or personal health facilities, or hiking, fishing and so on. The kernel is Kruger National Park's 19,000 square kilometres, two-thirds the size of Belgium or Massachusetts. To the west, it has already incorporated many abutting private game reserves, all of which have agreed to co-operate with South African National Parks' wildlife management regimen. This bloc has the potential to link with a chain of existing reserves to the west, all the way to the top of the Drakensberg escarpment. The idea is to consolidate them all into a band of unfenced protected areas and perhaps restore the ancient migration routes.

To the east of Kruger lies Mozambique's Parque Nacional do Limpopo (PNL, the Limpopo National Park). This has already been amalgamated with Kruger to form the Great Limpopo Transfrontier Park – a "peace park" that allows free travel throughout its 35,000 square kilometres on one passport. The Memorandum of Understanding for the creation of the peace park was signed on 10 November 2000, and the fences have come down, although neither Mozambique nor Zimbabwe has ratified the treaty. Potentially the international reserve could expand to almost 50,000 square kilometres – rivalling the world's biggest (Tanzania's Selous Game Reserve). However, even the current amalgamation seems premature, because neither Mozambique nor Zimbabwe is to be trusted with elephants. Mozambique is still a soft touch for ivory poaching – the corruption currently involves the police and government ministers. Zimbabwe's President Robert Mugabe, who has boasted of protecting a core population, "The President's Elephants", in Hwange National Park, allows various people to hunt them. Sharon Pincott in her 2016 book, *Elephant Dawn*, describes how, for years, as a researcher, she was encouraged to befriend a herd in Hwange – just as Jane Goodall spent years with Tanzania's chimpanzees in order to study their social habits. Then Pincott discovered the truth – whole herds were being poisoned with strychnine, and their tusks removed. Her "own" habituated community – supposedly under the protection of Mugabe – fled in terror at the faint sound of gunfire. Pincott left Zimbabwe fearing for her safety.

Don Pinnock of the online news service News 24 reported in December 2016 that the Mozambican section of the huge park had lost "more than half" its elephant population in five years. A Peace Parks technical adviser counted 66 live elephants and 53 carcasses in the Mozambican sector, and Michelle Henley of Elephants Alive flew over the northern sections and found no elephants at all.

Part of the problem, according to Pinnock, is that Kruger Park has concentrated its forces to the south to curb rhino poaching from Mozambique, leaving the central and north open to elephant poaching.

Other consolidations are progressing more smoothly.

The Addo Elephant National Park in the Eastern Cape has in recent years been extended to the Indian Ocean coast to become South Africa's third-largest park. It has incorporated adjacent private reserves within its ecosystem. Six hundred elephants now have a far wider range.

There is another developing belt of elephant country in South Africa's northeast corner: the 3,320 square kilometre iSimangaliso Wetland Park incorporates a couple of hundred kilometres of wild coast as well as Africa's biggest estuary, the dual saltwater/freshwater ecology of Lake St Lucia, along with Lake Sibaya, South Africa's largest freshwater lake, and a chain of four lakes in the Kosi Bay region on Mozambique's border. iSimangaliso has plans to amalgamate with game reserves in Mozambique and Swaziland, and its chief executive Andrew Zaloumis believes it will be possible to allow animals to migrate between the Indian Ocean coast and the forested Lebombo Mountains to the west.

It is within the realms of possibility to link iSimangaliso Wetland Park, via Mozambique's reserves, right up to Kenya and Tanzania – a concept first articulated by the South African statesman, Jan Christiaan Smuts, in the 1930s. When Richard Leakey revisited South Africa in 1984 after apartheid ended, I was asked to formally introduce him to the annual meeting of the Institute for the Study of Man in Africa. I mentioned the idea of a strip of reserves up to Kenya. I mentioned that there'd be no need to displace people, because the park could incorporate existing villages and towns, involving local people in the tourism industry. Leakey's reaction was unexpected. He said, "We don't want to be stared at like animals!" He'd obviously not visited areas such as England's Cotswolds, where half the charm is in the countryside and the other half lies in the villages, towns and people.

The mooted Kavango-Zambezi Transfrontier Conservation Area – the Kaza Park – could, eventually, amalgamate reserves from the Atlantic to the Indian oceans, offering opportunities for safari lodges, wildlife viewing, birding, hiking, motoring, hunting and fishing (freshwater and marine). The reserve incorporates what is currently marginal and agriculturally non-productive land. It is a characteristic of game reserves that they mostly comprise land that is only marginally suited for other uses. Only more recently have protected areas been aligned with areas of high biodiversity value.

There has also been talk in the Peace Parks Foundation – though nothing more than that so far – of joining the huge Selous Game Reserve in Tanzania to Mozambique's Niassa National Reserve on the other side of the Rufiji River, as mentioned in Chapter Four.

Thus a contiguous band of wild country could one day stretch along almost the entire sub-Saharan eastern flank of Africa, to preserve the last sustainable vestige of the Pleistocene's megafauna. It would also help create a zone that would be able to withstand the increasingly evident impacts of climate changes (such as severe droughts and floods). It would offer opportunities to communities to engage in the globally promising green economy by providing a diversity of livelihoods beyond what cattle and agriculture can provide, as climate change gains momentum.

6 Rhino –
e is for extinction

I have plucked the horn from the
saucy nose of the Rhinoceros.

William Cornwallis Harris (1840)

**It is a miracle that this prehistoric
idiot still exists.**

T. Murray Smith, *The Nature of the Beast* (1963)

On the night of 11 April 2013, three men entered Dublin's
National Museum, tied up the night watchman and stole
four African rhino heads from a storeroom. The heads had
been moved from public display by the museum for safety.

At the time, rhino horn was fetching $65,000/kilogram on
the black market; the Dublin haul weighed 10 kilograms. The
illicit trade in rhino horn had become more lucrative than the
drug trade; weight for weight, rhino horn was more valuable
than gold, platinum or cocaine.

By the following year, dozens of museums across Europe
had removed their rhino heads from public display. Others
put up notices advising visitors that the real horns had been
replaced by replicas. Sixty museums, from Norway to Italy,
did not react in time and lost their rhino horns; often other
precious exhibits were stolen *en passant*.

In 2014, Austrian police, investigating the theft of rhino
horns from a Vienna museum and from an antique dealer,

sought to extradite an Irish Traveller to face charges. In my childhood in the Staffordshire/Warwickshire countryside, Travellers were known as Gypsies or Tinkers. They are a nomadic and flamboyant people who have traditionally lived in ornately decorated horse-drawn caravans (but now favour modern motor-drawn caravan trailers).

Austria requested the Garda, Ireland's police force, to help track the wanted Traveller. As it turned out, the Garda had already arraigned him in Limerick, where he shared an address with a second suspect. The gardaí had also arrested another man, wanted by the British police after the theft of rhino horn from a Nottingham antique dealer.

When Europe's police started sharing their information, they noticed that nearly all the suspects were Irish; and the name Rathkeale, variously spelt, kept cropping up. Gradually they uncovered a gang of highly mobile Travellers. But these Travellers were using planes, not trailers, for their range now stretched as far as Australia. All hailed from the small town of Rathkeale in County Limerick, 80% of which had been bought up by the Travellers over the years. Some owned complete rows of houses, though police found many were empty and securely boarded up because the owners were either travelling around the world, or preferred sleeping in their caravans on the edge of town.

The gang, who became known as the "Rathkeale Rovers", specialised in stealing rhino horn from collections, and were also adept at stealing rare antiquities, often to order.

Ultimately 14 Rathkeale men were rounded up in the British Isles, convicted of possession or sale of rhino horn, and sentenced to terms ranging from five to seven years – the latter being the maximum sentence for smuggling. Of the many millions of dollars' worth of horn they'd stolen, only a third was retrieved. Considering the size of the prize, the criminals must have felt they had themselves a bargain.

In 2014 two Irishmen, arrested in the USA with rhino horn they'd bought illegally in Texas and were about to export to the Far East, were sentenced to 12 months and 14 months respectively. With good behaviour, they'd be out in no time, high-fiving and having a good laugh. Edward Grace, deputy assistant director for law enforcement at the US Fish and Wildlife Service in Washington, commented afterwards about the 15 kilogram horn they possessed: "By the time it gets to Asia, a single horn can easily be worth $500,000 ... (yet) a first-time offender would get off with less than a year, and, more likely, a fine. It's a high-profit, low-risk crime."

A lot of courts in the northern hemisphere, and even some in Africa, did not see the smuggling of wildlife parts as a particularly serious type of crime. In the Far East, the ransacking of Africa for ivory or rhino horn had long been of little concern to the receiving countries; China, for instance, banned the rhino-horn trade 30 years earlier, but the regulations were never taken seriously there. Even unprocessed horn was considered a good investment. However, China had more recently been strengthening relations with mineral-rich countries in Africa, and it was becoming uneasy about the morality of its role in poaching.

Slowly, surveillance in Europe and North America was stepped up, along with prison sentences. Later in 2014, the leader of an international crime ring trading in rhinoceros horn was jailed in the USA for almost six years after pleading guilty to charges of smuggling.

Rhino taxonomy

Rhinos have been around since the middle of the Miocene when the Andes Mountains were formed and East Africa's Great Rift Valley appeared. The Himalayas were still rising when the ancestral rhinos roamed.

During the Pleistocene there were several species, of which five survive: three in South Asia, and two in Africa.

Africa has the 2.5-tonne white rhino, *Ceratotherium simum,* and the 1.5-tonne black rhino, *Diceros bicornis.*

The three Asian species include the Javan rhino, *Rhinoceros sondaicus,* which is a little smaller than the African black rhino and is down to its last 60 individuals. It is, I suppose, the world's rarest species of megafauna. It is confined to western Java and its numbers recovered from fewer than 30 in 1967 to between 50 and 60 in 1980. Since then the population has been stagnant or even slowly declining. None have been re-established in the areas from which they were exterminated by hunting and loss of habitat. Like the two African variants but alone among the Asian species, the Javan rhino has two horns.

The Sumatran rhino, *Dicerorhinus sumatrensis,* is so hairy it is reminiscent of its extinct cousin, the woolly rhinoceros. It is the smallest of the rhinos (1.3 metres at shoulder height) and weighs 750 kilograms on average, though exceptional specimens may exceed a tonne.

It is rare because it lives on islands, which makes any animal vulnerable, and its habitat is confined to small forest patches at high altitudes. Poaching and loss of habitat have reduced it to about 275 specimens, though it appears to be holding its own in small, scattered, protected areas and in captive breeding programmes under armed patrols. A few years ago one was seen in the Kalimantan forests of north Borneo (part of Malaysia), where it had been considered extinct for 40 years.

The Indian rhinoceros, *Rhinoceros unicornis* – also called the greater one-horned rhinoceros – is native to the Indian subcontinent and is listed as "vulnerable". It is the second-largest living rhinoceros, and often exceeds 2 tonnes. Its heavily folded hide gives it the appearance of wearing overlapping armour plates and, if history is correct, the kings in ancient

India used it in warfare as a sort of front-line tank. In the early 1990s there were fewer than 2,000 alive; by 2015 their numbers in the wild had risen to 3,555.

Counting African rhinos

White rhino used to be common throughout sub-Saharan Africa, particularly in the grasslands of southern Africa. Strictly a grazer, it is usually seen head down out in the open; being quite bovine, it is neither very alert nor agile – a pathetically easy target for hunters. In 1836 the hunter-explorer William Cornwallis Harris saw 80 "in a day's march", a little north of where Johannesburg is today. Naturally, he shot everything he saw, which must have provided as much sport as shooting Jersey cows. Another hunter, Gordon-Cumming, also tended to shoot rhinos on sight – including one he shot just for lion bait. In 1873 F. C. Selous, hunting in Southern Rhodesia (now Zimbabwe) along the Limpopo and Chobe rivers, found many; but six years later, to his perplexity, he found none. He described a trading store that stocked a hundred or more horns for export to the Near East – mainly for turning into *jambiya* dagger handles, which at the time were a status symbol for young Yemenis. (Nowadays it's a Harley Davidson.) Boer hunters shot the rhino to use their hide for making *sjamboks*, heavy whips for driving draught oxen. Some hunters shot them merely for the nuchal hump – the white rhino's neck hump of fat and muscle tissue – which, baked in clay, is very palatable.

By the end of the century, when Selous was commissioned to collect one or two white rhinos for museums, he was unable to find a single specimen. Later, another hunter found what was perhaps the last bull in Southern Rhodesia, duly shot it and presented it to Cecil Rhodes for the Cape Town museum. Nowadays it is *really* protected, night and day.

Despite the heroic efforts of these hunters, some rhino did survive into the 20th century – mostly in northern KwaZuluNatal – but in the 1940s the government embarked on an ill-advised and catastrophic big-game extermination campaign in order to eradicate *ngana,* a cattle disease carried by the tsetse fly. This fly, which will not cross wide places in full sun, uses the shade beneath the bellies of wild mammals for transport. The campaign worked; *ngana* was eradicated – and so was the wildlife. The *ngana* campaign ecologically wrecked one of Africa's major, relatively unspoiled wildlife areas. Vast numbers of buffalo, elephant, antelope and other creatures were shot out of hand, in one of the lowest points of South Africa's conservation history.

In the IUCN's 1999 report on the status of the white rhino, it was claimed that as few as 20 had survived the 1930s massacre. It was often asserted that even in the 1950s there were only 40–80 southern white rhinoceroses left in the world – all of them in Zululand's iMfolozi Game Reserve in the northern part of KwaZulu-Natal. I confess to having used such figures myself, not knowing any better, and I have never been corrected – which is surprising, because in fact there were far more than that.

Ian Player, who was to become conservator for Zululand and whose 'Operation Rhino' is credited with saving the white rhino from extinction, performed a three-day fixed-wing aerial count in 1953 that found 437 animals in the park. It was Player's initiative that was to save the white rhino and give hope to all who were, and still are, striving to stabilise the world's beleaguered megafauna.

In 1964 the IUCN launched its Red List, which categorises the conservation status of various species worldwide. It listed the white rhino as EN – for "endangered". The animal seemed lined up for the penultimate category: CR – "critically endangered". The next category is E – and E is for "extinct".

Yet 50 years later, at the dawn of the current century, there were, once more, thousands roaming the savanna in many parts of Africa as well as thriving in safari parks and breeding zoos across America and Europe. This stands as a massive vindication of those optimistic conservationists, fund-raisers, NGOs and government departments who worked to re-establish a species teetering on the edge of oblivion. Although in the 1950s the white rhino's survival seemed far from secure, in 1997 the IUCN estimated that, after years of protection and many translocations, there were now 8,440 re-established in 247 locations, with a further 650 in captivity. The white was now the most numerous of the world's five extant rhinoceros species. The IUCN said its recovery was "recognised as one of the world's greatest conservation successes". For all that, the white rhino is still listed as "near threatened" on the IUCN Red List.

In the 1930s a last, lone black rhino was spotted in Kruger. Thanks to Operation Rhino there are now 600.

There were about 65,000 black rhino in Africa in 1960, but by 1993 they were down 96% to around 2,300. Today there are about 5,000 black and 20,000 white rhinoceroses in sub-Saharan Africa – 75% of them in South Africa, with the rest thinly scattered. Twenty-three countries that once had rhino no longer have any.

The white rhinoceros

I first became interested in the white rhino's story when the animal was still confined to the iMfolozi Game Reserve – a former Zulu hunting ground where, even now, one stumbles across the bush-choked pits dug by the Zulu in the 19th century to trap large animals like rhino. The description "white" has nothing to do with its colour or lack of it; just like its "black" cousin, the "white" rhino is unequivocally grey. The name derives from the old Dutch word *weid*, describing the animal's wide mouth. Also known as the "square-lipped" rhino, it's an enormous grass-cutting machine whose wide lips are rivalled only by that other massive grazer, the hippopotamus.

The white rhino's ferocious reputation is hardly justified. I watched a ranger in Zululand, for a dare, creep up behind one and slap it on the rump to send it snorting away. However, I also recall a ranger being killed by one – one of only four fatalities related to white rhinos of which I am aware.

The northern race of the white rhino, *Ceratotherium simum cottonii*, used to be found 4,000 kilometres to the north; a lot of the heads stolen from Europe's museums belonged to this species, mostly originating from Sudan, where the animal has long been extinct.

In 1960 there were an estimated 2,250 in northern Africa. In 1975, when there were probably still about 1,000 northern whites, a plan was hatched to revive the species in their last known habitat, the savanna in the northeastern corner of the Democratic Republic of the Congo and adjacent states. It came to nothing amid wrangling and internecine regional wars. The Congolese killed most of the last few hundred to raise money for weapons. Unlike the northern rhino, the wars go on.

By the year 2000 there were only 25 northern white rhino, and the last known young male in the wild died in 2006. In 2015, the last northern bull died of natural causes in the Ol Pejeta Conservancy in Kenya, where the last half-dozen had been brought for safety. There are now four individuals left corralled there – all females. Extinction is assured.

I was fortunate enough to meet Ian Player and witness the success of the conservation efforts for the southern white rhino. This came about indirectly through our 1960s involvement with *Rhino!*, a rather forgettable film offering a dose of romance in the thornveld. I had been invited by the Hollywood film producer, Ivan Tors, to join him and his crew in Zululand, where they were hoping to repeat their recent success with *Lawrence of Arabia.*

My role was to write for various American publications about the making of the film and about the brand-new science of big-game immobilisation and translocation. I stayed with the crew (the cast comprised Shirley Eaton, Harry Guardino and Bob Culp) at Mpila Camp, which is on a high ridge overlooking the iMfolozi River's long and beautiful valley. Tors gave me the script to read; it gave a starring role to the white rhino, which the Hollywood scriptwriter had assumed to be like the black rhino, irascible and dangerous. I explained to Tors that (bar the tortoises), the white rhino was about the most amiable animal in the bush, and was unlikely to act the part he expected of it. He got around this difficulty by mounting a full-scale model of a white rhino head on the end of a pole; an assistant, with a camera following, manipulated this in all sorts of aggressive actions, including chasing a man up a tree. Then Tors bought some footage of a *black* rhino attacking a vehicle. One scene in the movie shows a small herd of white rhino reacting to the camera; one of them ambles a few steps away from the herd towards the camera. Suddenly, the rhino appears to charge the vehicle and do some serious panelbeating. In a blur of motion, the white rhino had become a black one, but few filmgoers noticed the switch.

During the filming I got to know Ian Player who, as chief ranger, had a house a short walk from Mpila Camp. We were to become lifelong friends. Like his brother Gary Player, one of history's greatest golfers, Ian, who died in 2015, was a single-minded individual. As a raw game ranger in the mid-1950s he had seen the opportunity to re-establish the white rhino throughout its former range. He was aware that his little-known provincial game reserve had no state protection and could be deproclaimed any time, though it was just about the only remaining sanctuary for the world's second-largest land mammal, which had been extinct in the Kruger National Park since 1896. The white rhinoceros had no nationally protected area. The species was extremely vulnerable and, as Player put it, "Here we were with all our eggs in one basket!"

Operation Rhino

When Player was promoted to senior ranger, he approached the Natal Parks Board and proposed "Operation Rhino". Its aim was simple – to re-establish the white rhino in its old haunts and to get as many eggs out of that one basket and dispersed as soon as possible. There was very little money for conservation in the sixties. Nor was there any help or enthusiasm coming from the central government, which was preoccupied with breaking up South Africa into racially separate regions. As a result of this apartheid policy, South Africa was being internationally boycotted, so there seemed no hope of overseas funding. Yet, as Player's plan unfolded, he began to gain many allies – especially American and German big-game hunters. Player, who spoke colloquial Zulu, was no apologist for apartheid. He often travelled with his personable mentor, Maqubu Nthombela, a wise and gentle Zulu who spoke no English. No matter how "posh" the hotel in which the two stayed, Maqubu insisted on going to the kitchen and cooking his own, very basic, food in a three-legged iron pot that travelled everywhere with him.

I was sworn to secrecy many times in the early days of Operation Rhino. Player was distributing rhinos across Africa – even to countries that had declared at the UN that they had severed all trade and diplomatic ties with South Africa. Many of the animals were destined for breeding in zoos (which many conservationists would not have liked); but the San Diego Zoo, for instance, an early beneficiary, now has a large herd and sells its surplus.

Though Player was not a hunter, he was never against hunting, and he was well aware that it was hunters who had pressed for the establishment of the Kruger Park at the end of the 19th century. They realised game was fast diminishing, and a protected reservoir of big game was in their interest. And it was hunters, not conservationists, who had helped save millions of square kilometres of North America's wetland – mainly so that they could continue to shoot ducks. Yet the gun-toting members of Ducks Unlimited used only 10% of the land, leaving the rest available for public use. Player pragmatically wooed the hunting lobby, who became powerful allies as he toured America – where his brother was already very popular – and helped him find many backers.

Once the Natal Parks Board gave Player the go-ahead to launch "Operation Rhino" in the late 1950s, he set about rescuing the rhino from extinction. His plan was to immobilise the animals and transport them, under sedation, first to Kruger National Park (until breeding nuclei were established) and then wherever there was suitable habitat or breeding opportunities. Politics and boycotts were immaterial to him – his only concern was to find nations prepared to accept, under the counter if necessary, a breeding pair or herd.

Neither he nor his team had any training in game capture, or knowledge of immobilising agents and techniques for use on large animals.

In 1959 I was invited by the National Parks Board to witness the first attempt at heavy game capture in South Africa, which was to take place on the Olifants River in Kruger Park. The river was very low at the time and it had become expedient to try to move some hippos to a less drought-stricken area. The hippopotamus, when fully grown, is about the same weight as a rhino, but it is a very nasty adversary at close quarters – far more dangerous than any other large animal. The attempt nearly ended in tragedy, but a lot was learned from it. A likely hippo was spotted 50 metres out in midstream and everybody – there were a dozen of us – had a go at estimating its weight. We settled on 500 kilograms. Establishing the animal's weight was important in order to judge the dose of Sernyl (Phencyclidine – the immobilising agent) that was to be injected via a hollow dart delivered by a gas-propelled gun. Sernyl was developed in the 1950s as an intravenous anaesthetic for humans but withdrawn from use – it made people hallucinate – and restricted to the veterinary field.

A vet carefully measured the dose and syringed it into the dart. The missile was fired, and the animal barely reacted as the dart pierced its flank. Minutes later, the hippo became still, half-floating in a metre or so of water. Ranger Piet Barnard waded out to it with a noose to pull it ashore, from where it was to be loaded into a truck lined with mattresses. As he tried to place the noose around its huge neck the hippo suddenly raised its head and bit Barnard across his torso, its enormous tusks bouncing off his hips and raising a huge weal. It then bit through his armpit and shoulder before a ranger killed it with two rapid shots from a heavy-calibre rifle. The nearest hospital was hours away, but the badly injured Barnard survived and was back on duty within weeks. It turned out the hippo weighed a tonne – twice our estimate.

Player's method likewise involved guessing the target animal's weight in order to prepare, as precisely as possible, a cocktail of Sernyl and Hyaluronidase – the latter to speed up the drug's absorption. He would stand in the back of an open Land Rover, holding on to the roll bar with one hand, capture gun in the other, and look out for a rhino, often a member of a small herd. He'd indicate the target animal to the ranger at the wheel, who would then cautiously edge the vehicle towards the herd. Once the herd broke into a gallop – and rhinos, despite their characteristic bouncing gait, can move at 25 kilometres/hour – the driver would accelerate to keep pace alongside the target animal. At a range of 2 metres Player, or the shooter on duty, would fire into its rump. The rhino would gallop blindly off on its own and the vehicle would stop as two mounted rangers, who had been following close behind, thundered past the vehicle to follow the animal. The drug's knockdown time was 20 minutes, sometimes more. Later a synthetic morphine, M99, was developed that reduced the knockdown time to nine minutes.

The chase entailed crashing through thorn thickets. The horses wore protective skirts but rangers soon learned to discard their shirts because it was easier to patch up their skin than sew up a shredded shirt. When the rhino faltered and eventually went down, one of the riders would radio the back-up vehicle, bearing its stout wooden crate, and guide it in. The vet would then inject Lethidrone, an antidote to the immobilising drug, into an ear vein – just enough to enable the dazed animal to stagger to its feet and allow half a dozen men to push and pull it into the crate. It would then be transported, under sedation, to a holding *boma* (a stout enclosure made of logs) while it recovered before being transported to its new location. The top 16cm of its horn was taken off by a buzz-saw, and sometimes left in the veld. The capture process was a rough-and-ready method and not without its accidents, some quite serious – but it worked. Interestingly, white rhino, though quite passive compared with the black, were much less tractable once enclosed in a *boma* than the traditionally short-tempered black. The black – more intelligent perhaps? –

seemed to learn quite quickly that humans meant them no harm, and they were quicker to accept a pat on the head.

Tony Harthoorn of University College, Nairobi, an extraordinary man and a pioneer of big-game immobilisation with five earned PhDs, arrived to help with the chemistry. Judging the animal's weight was a critical part of the procedure, but it was a very inexact science. On seeing his first southern white rhino, he asked Player its weight. "Three tonnes," said Player. Most rangers thought a fully grown rhino would easily tip 3,000 kilograms. The first rhino targeted, although it received the dose that all had carefully agreed upon, never stopped running, and the rangers eventually gave up the chase. The next went down after a few minutes and never got up.

This was alarming. Here was one of the rarest animals on Earth, for which American zoos (which helped finance Operation Rhino) would pay thousands of dollars each; and the rangers had no idea of how to calculate the correct dose. When Harthoorn established that the overdosed animal was dead, he immediately ordered saws, axes, buckets and scales. He then supervised the rapid dismemberment of the rhinoceros and the weighing of all its body parts and fluids. Later, covered in gore, filth and perspiration, the team was astonished at the rhino's weight – just over two tonnes.

Later it was agreed that a fully grown bull rhino is unlikely to exceed 2.5 tonnes.

Harthoorn began a series of trial-and-error attempts to bring the animals down as quickly but as gently as possible. There were no further fatal overdoses, but captured rhinos continued to die. While in iMfolozi I shared a chalet with Keith Ditman, a Beverley Hills expert on psychotropic drugs who counted Marilyn Monroe among his patients. He was there to advise the MGM crew. As we discussed the rhino deaths one evening, Ditman asked me if I had noticed what "sterile technique" rangers were using. "How do they clean the needles?" he asked. I said, "I think they just wipe them." Next morning, he put the question to Player, who confirmed they wiped used needles with their fingers before reusing them. "It's septicaemia," said Ditman. "That's what's killing them". There were no more mysterious deaths after that.

The first captured white rhinos arrived in the Kruger Park in June 1962. By September 1964 there were just short of 100. Most did well, though they soon encountered some dangerous and unfamiliar neighbours that had long been extinct in Zululand. An adult male was killed by lions, and one newcomer, near Shingwedzi in the north of the park, failed to give way to an elephant. The surrounding spoor revealed the two had become engaged in mortal combat that had ended when they both fell down a 30-metre embankment, whereupon the elephant settled the argument by twice impaling the rhino on its tusks.

Though poaching continues to increase throughout Africa – more than 1,000 rhino a year have been poached since 2012, and 2015 reached a new record of 1,338 – the park's rhino population was officially estimated in 2016 at "between 8,400 and 9,300 individuals".

White rhino were also sent, secretly, to officially hostile African states, as well as Southern Rhodesia (now Zimbabwe), where they bred well; but poaching has since almost returned them to extinction there.

Today the white rhino as a species is safe; 20,000 of these pachyderms are now re-established in areas where they'd been extinct for a century and more. Breeding herds are widely spread. It is the first mammal to be removed from the IUCN's Red Data Endangered Species list. Ironicallly, iMfolozi itself is today overstocked with white rhino.

The black rhinoceros

At the time of Operation Rhino, South Africa's population of black rhino was down to about 400 in widely scattered locations. One highly secret move involved Kenya, which officially and ostentatiously shunned all public contact with South Africa in the apartheid era. Player managed to swop six of iMfolozi's white rhino for six of Kenya's black rhino – destined for Kruger Park where they were long extinct. At that time Kenya had about 20,000 black rhino. However, when Kenya's black rhino arrived it was realised they were *Diceros bicornis minor* – a subspecies of southern Africa's *D. bicornis,* and therefore could not be released into the wild. They were accommodated separately in the ideal habitat of Addo Elephant National Park in the Eastern Cape, where today there are about three dozen. An agreement was reached that they would all one day be returned to Kenya, whose black rhino population has meanwhile been reduced to 540 through poaching.

The black rhinoceros is rather myopic, which is probably why it is more alert than its cousins. It is inclined to defend itself by attacking, or at least putting on a threatening display. Its myopia is such that it can mistake a car for a mate, and it has been known to put on quite an enthusiastic mating performance until it detects a certain lack of enthusiasm in the vehicle's reaction; then it may ram the unwilling partner, or try to dismantle it, before moving off with its tail curled up in disgust. At 1.5 tonnes, it greatly exceeds the weight of even a big car.

Like all browsers, the black rhino holds its head high. Its head is much smaller than the white's and its mouth is pointed, with a prehensile upper lip to facilitate grasping and biting shrubbery. It prefers thick bush, and its only association with its big and distant cousin of the open plains is that it sometimes deposits its droppings on top of the white rhino's midden. A well-used white rhino midden resembles several wheelbarrow-loads of fine, brown grass mowings, often dry and soft enough to use for stuffing pillows (almost). The difference between the two types of dung is easy to spot: the black rhino's droppings are made up of tiny sections of twigs, each neatly clipped off at a 45-degree angle.

Although the black rhino has indeed killed people over the years, its reputation as one of the most dangerous animals in the bush has been greatly exaggerated. Hunters have long argued over its position in "the Big Five" – the five most dangerous animals to hunt. The five are lion, leopard, elephant, *black* rhino and buffalo. Some argue, unconvincingly, they would rather run into a lion, a leopard, or even a buffalo or elephant, than a black rhino. At least those animals prefer flight to fight. When the black rhino suspects somebody is nearby, it tends to spin around and advance, hesitantly at first, towards the source of its irritation. It will then stop and listen, swivelling its funnel-like ears and sniffing the air with distended nostrils. If the person remains still, it will probably saunter off. On the other hand it might decide to charge. Black rhino have been known to charge trucks, and one in Kenya took on a locomotive; it was killed on impact.

C. A. W. Guggisberg, the East African wildlife writer, points out that many people who claim to have been charged by black rhinos have merely been the subject of an "exploratory advance." In *Man is the Prey* I wrote of the belief of many big-game hunters that one can simply sidestep a charging black rhinoceros, which will go trundling past, and eventually stop and begin browsing again. Jim Feely, a colleague of Ian Player and an authority on rhinos, used to stand his ground when a black rhino charged him and, as it reached him, would turn it with a whack across the nose from his rifle butt. I imagine that takes very precise timing and a very cool nerve.

Player knew of a few men killed by black rhino over the years. He said, "I doubt whether there is a game ranger in these parts who has not been charged by one", and did not advise trying to sidestep a charge. "The only sensible thing to do when confronted by a charging rhino", he advised, "is find a tree and climb it – even 4 foot (say shoulder height) is usually safe enough." Failing that, he said, "sometimes, the best trick is to chuck your hat or bush jacket – or anything – in its way and hope it will take it out on that."

The poachers and the rangers

Stealing the relics of long-dead animals from museums is one thing; coming to Africa to obliterate living rhinos – a species that plays a leading role in Africa's tourist-attracting, self-renewing, $80 billion a year wildlife show, is quite another. In South Africa, for example, wildlife is the fifth biggest sector in the agricultural industry and earns R9 billion a year.

Up to 2007, South Africa was losing a dozen or so rhino a year to poachers. But in 2008, 100 were killed; in 2010, 333 (including 10 black rhino); and the numbers have been increasing exponentially year by year. In 2012, the Kruger Park alone lost 1,215 rhino. Private owners began to sell off their rhino; the cost of protecting them, which entails 24-hour patrols and costly electric fencing, had become too great. And the violence was escalating too. The South African Private Rhino Owners' Association claims 220 poachers were killed between 2008 and 2015. In 2015, 20 poachers were killed in Kruger Park alone, and nine were wounded. Rhino poaching had become a war, fought by locally recruited mercenaries on behalf of Asian businessmen and, by default, on behalf of the Vietnamese and Chinese governments. The Asian syndicates were now equipping their proxies with helicopters, rapid-firing rifles, and guns with silencers and night-vision attachments.

Most of the Kruger Park poachers – who were killing two or three rhinos a night – were coming from the underdeveloped area along the Olifants valley in Mozambique, where poaching is the region's major source of income. The incentives are enormous. A kilogram of rhino horn would fetch $65,000 and sometimes more. The two horns of an average-sized rhino can weigh almost 6 kilograms – that's $400,000. The front horn of a prize white rhino can grow to more than 1.5 metres – $1,000,000 worth of keratin.

Over a two-year period, security forces arrested 379 poachers, some of whom went to prison for 16 years. One, convicted of murder along with his other crimes, got a 77-year sentence.

Prince Harry, the Queen's grandson, spent three months in South Africa in 2016 looking at its wildlife situation. He joined night patrols into Kruger Park attached to South Africa's "Operation Corona", a government-financed initiative involving the army, navy, air force, police and paramilitary rangers. Corona is intended to stop incursions like those on the Mozambique border, which were costing South Africa R228 million a year – not counting the value of the game that was being poached or the long-term damage to the tourist trade. The Corona team includes the intelligence units of the police and army as well as the National Prosecuting Authority and magistrates, who are invited to meetings so that they can appreciate their role in handing out appropriate sentences.

Drones are used to scan the park's vast, complex terrain. Normally the hunt for poachers on the ground is left to rangers with dogs, carrying flares to signal for a standby helicopter.

As many as 40 poachers, operating in teams of three, enter the park nightly. Some are former soldiers, and carry automatic assault rifles and grenades. Some are unemployed young men desperate enough to risk their lives to make the money to send their children to school; some are dangerous criminals.

Each team has a sniper who shoots the rhino and might get up to R500,000 for it. His two accomplices get as much R250,000 each. Each poacher gets an upfront deposit from the Far Eastern syndicates.

A 2016 WWF report revealed the skulduggery going on in Mozambique:

"Mozambique is ... a major exit point for rhino horn leaving the African continent en route to Asia. The Standing Committee of CITES requested Mozambique to develop and implement a detailed national rhino action plan. Despite these measures, rhino poaching and horn trafficking remain serious problems, as exemplified by a seizure of 65 rhino horns and 1.1 tonnes of elephant ivory in May 2015, following a police raid in Maputo. Subsequently, 12 rhino horns from this seizure were stolen from a police storeroom and at least seven individuals, four of them police officers, [were] arrested in connection with the theft. However, in July 2015 the Mozambican authorities destroyed the confiscated ivory and rhino horn before any cases in connection with the events had come to court."

In 2013, 30 of the 100 game rangers on the Mozambique side of the Great Limpopo Transfrontier Park were arrested for guiding poachers to the last elephants and rhinos. In the same year, the rhino was said to be extinct in Mozambique.

South Africa has begun to consider re-erecting the 30 kilometres of border fence that was taken down years ago. But it seems the enemy is already within the gates. According to the South African Army's *Defence* magazine, "the criminals have infiltrated our forces. Within two months we had over 56 arrests, but the dockets got lost. Once the dockets have gone missing, the case is over and the suspects are released". South African soldiers, camped on the border, have been known to help the poachers.

In March 2015 Bartholomaus Grill of the weekly German news magazine *Der Spiegel* and his Swedish photographer Toby Selander attempted to follow the supply chain that was moving the horns from South Africa, via middlemen in Mozambique, on to the buyers in Vietnam.

Grill easily tracked down the poaching kingpin "Navara" to his ostentatious house in Massingir close to the South African border; the town is also home to another 20-odd "poaching bosses". The local people are poor farmers and most of the young men are unemployed. Navara, who takes his nom de guerre from his favoured 4x4 vehicle, is "the most notorious of the lot, but everyone acts as though they had never heard the name".

Once the journalists found his house, they were quickly surrounded by a mob and accused of being South African spies. After a two-and-a-half hour interrogation by Navara and his men at a police station, they were told they were to be separated and taken to police headquarters in Massingir "to be locked away". As Grill reports: "We protest to the village policeman. Navara growls, 'I'm in command here!'"

The journalists were released only after the German and Swedish embassies asked the regional police chief about the men's whereabouts. He received the calls while interrogating them in his office, and had them escorted out of the region.

A security consultant, whose company has collected information about Navara for a client, claimed that he "is protected at the highest levels of government and by police leaders" who shield him from extradition to South Africa. Grill reports: "One witness watched as Navara walked into the local branch of Banco Comercial with bulging shopping bags filled with US banknotes. Rhino dollars."

Grill describes the web of corruption that sustains the trade: "... the raiding parties (of poachers) are only a small part of a much broader network that includes corrupt rangers, park officials, police officers, professional hunters and bush pilots. Game wardens are bribed to monitor the movements of the rhinoceros herds while veterinarians supply M99, an anaesthetic. Local politicians, safari organisers, cattle traders and white farmers act as go-betweens.

"The gang leaders are one rung further up the ladder. They sell the horns to smuggling rings that then bribe shipping companies, customs inspectors, port officials and airport personnel. Ministry employees and diplomats are often part of the criminal network. Indeed, workers at the Vietnamese Embassy ensure that the product makes its way to wholesalers in their homeland. South Africa has repeatedly launched investigations into suspect diplomats."

Grill adds that "Massingir District's economic potential is in fact enormous", with agriculture as well as tourism opportunities capable of lifting the locals out of poverty. It seems possible that tourism might one day persuade the Mozambique government to protect rhino, if only for economic reasons.

Soon after the Navara episode, it was reported that 12 rhino horns had been stolen from a police warehouse in Maputo. Four policemen were arrested and a senior officer was accused of being a ringleader. The president of Mozambique, Filipe Nyussi, commented rather unconvincingly: "When policemen are involved in trafficking rhinoceros horns, tusks and drugs, I cannot sleep".

The tourists

The slaughter of rhinos presents an obvious threat to the future of eco-tourism in Africa, by threatening to destroy this iconic species forever. Perhaps less obvious is the threat posed by the inevitable militarisation of the parks. Just how badly it is spoiling the tourists' experience was described to me by Glenn Havemann, who, with his wife – both are keen photographers – joined a three-day wilderness walk in 2016 with a party of six, accompanied by three rangers, along the Napi Trail in the south of Kruger Park. So popular are these walks that one has to book a year ahead. "Yes, we enjoyed it – we always do", said Havemann. "But ... one sees the occasional army vehicle and even an armed foot patrol. It's unfortunately necessary but it tarnishes the image of wild Africa.

"At the camps there have always been large maps at the shop entrances inviting visitors to use colour-coded pins to indicate where, that day, they'd seen lion or elephant or whatever. But no longer are there pins for rhino. We were told this was because Far Eastern spies, posing as tourists, are on the lookout for rhinos and tip off poachers via their cellphones.

"Worse, once on the trail we were constantly hearing and seeing helicopters – they sometimes came close to check if we were indeed tourists."

Foreign tourists are a little nervous of walking in wild Africa in the first place – but the thought of there being armed poachers about makes them even more so. Letters in travel magazines indicate some are saying "never again".

The consumers

It is worth considering exactly why rhino horn is considered so desirable by Far Eastern consumers.

According to statistics supplied by Tom Milliken of TRAFFIC, Japan was the main buyer throughout the 1970s, but demand reduction strategies worked, and that country is no longer a problem. South Korea and Taiwan remained major consumers until the early 1990s, when the threat of

US sanctions under the so-called "Pelly Amendment" was sufficient to kill the trade there.

The global trade generally slackened off until 2005, when Vietnam's economy reached new heights and it became the world's biggest buyer of South African rhino horn (both legal and illegal). It also became a major conduit for China, a country which claimed to have been complying with the CITES rhino horn ban since the 1980s.

Vietnam's growing affluent class believe powdered horn cures just about everything: fever, hangovers, impotence, cancer and ageing; and we can add status anxiety to this list, as just being able to flash a rhino horn is regarded as a sign of great wealth. The Chinese, on the other hand, contrary to popular Western belief, have never regarded it as an aphrodisiac or a cancer cure. However, for the past 2,000 years Chinese medical books have been recommending rhino horn potions for fever and heart problems, and many Chinese still believe this works.

Rhino horn is pure keratin – the same substance as fingernails, feathers and hooves. It can have no medicinal effects at all; and even those who believe otherwise can save themselves a lot of money by just chewing their own nails.

However, Gao Yufang, a doctoral student in anthropology at Yale writing in *Biological Conservation*, believes the Far Eastern market is being driven not by neurotics, but by investors, and thus efforts to steer people away from buying rhino horn (and ivory) should be focused on the arts and antiquities market, the auction houses and antique dealers. Ivory and horn objets d'art go back centuries in Chinese culture, which is noted for exquisite and intricate carvings. Some pieces fetch as much as Old Masters do in the West. Gao says that with the quite rapid emergence of an affluent middle class in China and Vietnam, people are looking for tangible investments as a hedge against inflation and for gifts to display their wealth. The Western media's emphasis on the supposed "medicinal" uses is therefore misplaced.

He supports this conclusion with an analysis of Eastern and Western press reports on the rhino horn situation between 2000 and 2014. Of 166 articles in British and American newspapers, he found that 84% emphasised the medicinal use of horn, while only 6% mentioned its investment value. In the East, of 332 newspapers surveyed, 79% wrote of the investment aspect while only 29% mentioned the medicinal applications.

Legalising the trade

There are more than 300 private breeders of white rhinos in South Africa, and they claim to own about a third of the country's rhino. The biggest of them, John Hume, has 1,400 on his 8,000ha ranch in the North West Province. He spends R2 million a month just to protect them, and claims he breeds them to create a repository to ensure the animal's survival. He made a strong but unsuccessful bid at the 2016 CITES meeting to reopen the horn trade with the East. His plan was to dehorn the live animals – their horns would grow again. Had his bid succeeded, his stock would have been worth almost $100 million (R1,4 billion at the time).

In February 2017 the wealthy Private Rhino Owners' Association persuaded the Ministry of Environmental Affairs to draft legislation allowing domestic, as opposed to international, trading, in rhino horn; though there is no evidence that South Africans are interested in possessing rhino horns. The department wished to treat rhino horn as a commodity, like wine or metal. Don Pinnock, the conservation specialist of the online news service *Daily Maverick*, noted

that the department had crossed the thin line between conservation and marketing:

"Ignoring the findings of environmental organisations, its
contractual compliance with CITES, a worldwide online
petition and its own strategic plan for rhinos, the Department
of Environmental Affairs (DEA) is about to open the door to
the commodification of rhino horn ...", wrote Pinnock,
pointing out that the department had previously opposed the
legalisation of the trade at the CITES CoP17 meeting in
Johannesburg and in the Constitutional Court.

Now it was proposing to legalise the (almost nonexistent)
"internal" trade and to allow every individual to buy, own,
sell or export (under CITES permit) two rhino horns. The
new regulations would apply to both black and white rhinos,
despite their very different conservation status. Their proper
application would require a raft of DNA, microchip and
document checking, which the DEA has no hope of adminis-
tering. As the conservationist Ian Michler explained: "There
is no realistic way of ensuring that the two horns per person
do not end up being traded."

The minister seemed reluctant to discuss the reasons for
the policy about-turn, which came hot on the heels of another
proposal by the DEA: the sale of lion bones, used in the
manufacture of fake tiger-bone wine (See Chapter 4).

The whole business is highly suspect and not well researched by the government, which patently has never been
able to control the trade, and will have even less chance of
doing so now. The most likely consequence is that lucrative
new channels would be opened up for laundering horns into
international markets. Vietnam's rhino horn merchants must
have been delighted.

Now, the biggest question of all is whether South Africa
will betray the world's conservation movement and propose

full international trade in rhino horn at the next CITES conference in 2019.

On the other hand – what if Vietnam and China cease trading in horn, rendering it worthless?

7 The sea – the last resource

Roll on, thou deep and dark-blue Ocean, roll!
Ten thousand fleets sweep over thee in vain;
Man marks the earth with ruin – his control
Stops with the shore; upon the watery plain
The wrecks are all thy deed, nor doth remain
A shadow of man's ravage.

George Gordon, Lord Byron (1818)

The 19th-century overkill was not confined to the land – eco-cide was just as bad in the seas. Marine life was so ripe for plundering. Patently Byron, like everyone else, was blissfully unaware of the extent to which "man's ravage" was happening even then. Whaling had long been a free-for-all in the North Atlantic; so much so that the British and Dutch whalers had noticed a fall-off in whale numbers and were now moving south. They were soon joined by others, but the pickings were slim. Then the American whaling fleets discovered the great plethora of sperm whales in the mid-Pacific. The tragedy of the ill-starred whaler, the *Essex*, inspired Herman Melville's *Moby Dick* and gave the world a glimpse of the reality of whaling, of killing 40-tonne mammals with hand-held harpoons from a wooden boat. Later, the harpoons were fitted with exploding heads and fired from cannons. So even the Pleistocene's mightiest survivors, the whales – the largest creatures ever to evolve – were now totally at our mercy. Their smaller cousins, the dolphins, so pathetically trusting of humans, were, in their turn, slaughtered indiscriminately.

In the 19th century, the world's human population was smaller than that of India today, and there was plenty of everything for everybody. There was no global conscience, no planetary patriotism and no interspecies ethics.

Under the sea, there is still much innocence in the animal world. I was snorkelling along the Great Barrier Reef some years ago and noticed how the shoals of fish barely moved out of the way. A nosy hawksbill turtle sidled up to investigate. Just as it was on land at the dawn of the Holocene, the animals had no fear of humans; a phenomenon I have also witnessed off the coasts of KwaZulu-Natal and Mozambique. I have swum with dolphins off Cape St Francis. They seemed filled with curiosity as they swam up to me and around me though not quite within touching distance. They even seemed playful.

Worldwide, the management of the sea's resources has an abysmal history. The Law of the Sea Convention of 1982, now ratified by 167 nations, was an important step forward; but as with the Convention on International Trade in Endangered Species (CITES), nations cheat – some of them outrageously.

The worldwide commercial catch, which stood at 21 million tonnes in 1950, reached a record level of 84.5 million tonnes in 1988 according to the Worldwatch Institute, but it has registered no notable change since then. This is not a good sign, as it seems that despite the arrival of more and more ships with better and better equipment, no more fish are to be found. Properly managed, the sustainable catch would probably be around 100 million tonnes. But when one considers that subsistence fishermen pull in unknown millions of tonnes, that many fleet owners falsify figures, and that some fishing boat crews dump a whole day's catch so that they still have a job tomorrow, it is clear that we are witnessing a marine overkill.

Pollution

To some, the oceans have become the final dumping ground.

Thor Heyerdahl wrote of the unbroken 2,250-kilometre belt of surface pollution that he encountered in 1969 when he was drifting across the Atlantic on his papyrus raft *Ra*. Several times the surface of the sea was so contaminated with oil that his crew could not dip their toothbrushes in it. About the same time, scientists were doing an exploratory dredge of the deepest part of the Atlantic – the 9-kilometre-deep Puerto Rican Trench east of the Caribbean. They were surprised to find a 12cm-long fish living at that depth; but they were even more shocked to find paint cans, old batteries and other junk.

In 2017, I made a visit with a photographer to Lake St Lucia in northern KwaZulu-Natal in search of a bird that is rare in southern Africa: the Eurasian oystercatcher. On a secluded beach, we found what we were looking for and captured a nice picture of it. However, when we looked closely, we found the bird was standing among dozens of tiny plastic fragments. In fact the high-tide mark for kilometres was outlined by millions of plastic fragments, and I wondered if there was a kilometre of shoreline, anywhere in the world, that was not contaminated by this "ring around the bath".

Well over 300 million tonnes of indestructible plastic were daily dumped in the sea in 2014. Research released in 2015 revealed there were more than 5 trillion pieces of plastic floating in the seas, many just crumbs, 5 millimetres and less across. Larger items are sometimes eaten by turtles and seals with fatal results. Countless tiny crumbs drift to the bottom, forming an artificial layer on the seabed. The environmental and health impacts of this have not been assessed. The industry itself is keeping its head down; a recent report by Martin R. Stuchtey of the McKinsey Centre for Business and Environment said, "the plastics industry is comprehensively failing to address these issues ... a wave of innovation is needed".

The oil and plastics industry has found that with relatively low oil prices, it is cheaper to convert new oil into plastic, rather than recover and recycle the hydrocarbons from plastic waste. There seems to be insufficient incentive to tackle the problem seriously. In its haste to keep up with demand, industry is cutting corners – often a recipe for disaster. This was illustrated by the Gulf of Mexico disaster in April 2010 when, through carelessness, a BP oil rig blew up and a billion litres of crude oil gushed from the seabed before the well was properly capped almost three months later. Years later, the gulf's coastal rim is still coated in gunk and what sea life was not killed in those thousands of square kilometres was horribly contaminated. But oil, at least, is biodegradable; most plastic is not.

Marine overkill

Just as the hunters of the 18th and 19th centuries felt the urge to massacre the world's plains game, so, a century later, did those who commercially fished the waters off Africa become caught up by a similar compulsion. Overkill has wrecked most of Africa's fish stocks.

Sylvia Earle is a much admired and tireless marine biologist who won fame after spending two weeks with an all-female study team in *Tektite II,* an undersea "bubble" in the Caribbean. In a 1996 publication, *Diving for Science*, she wrote of the culture of collecting "bushmeat" from the sea – just casually and continually scooping up organisms. Her studies triggered a lot of introspection, worldwide, on how we treat our coastal waters. We tend to "harvest" coastal waters with no thought of sustainability and, adding insult to injury, annually dump more than 300 million tonnes of junk and gunk into those same waters.

The rape of the seas

Fish species that were once commonplace at fishmongers have "collapsed" – to use the South African Department of Sea Fisheries' own word.

For decades, fishing fleets across the world exploited sea life with insufficient knowledge and enormous greed. The sea occupies 71% of the Earth's surface, but it is very difficult to keep tabs on what is going on beneath the waves. The way the sea has been exploited could be likened to farming the land from above an impenetrable layer of cloud, blindly using fleets of wildly firing gunships and bombers to destroy the practically defenceless life below.

Each year the Atlantic has yielded millions of tonnes of fish; and properly managed, the North Atlantic could produce far more nutrition than the whole world's grain harvest. But it has been poorly regulated and poorly patrolled.

The sardine crash

An ocean of particular interest to Africa is the South Atlantic. Colossal damage was done in the 1960s and 1970s when the world's fishing nations descended on the sardine (pilchard) shoals off the continent's southwest coast. The sardines' sustenance came from the strong upwellings created by the Benguela Current surging north from the Antarctic. Those massive shoals included anchovies, and they represent to the sea's ecology what the plains game represents to the land's predators. They are basic to the survival of the marine megafauna – not just to the large species of fish, such as sharks and barracuda, but also to its mammals: seals and dolphins.

The sardine shoals off Namibia, properly managed, could have sustainably yielded 2 million tonnes a year. Instead they were destroyed by a period of overkill, driven by an unmitigated greed that is hard to fathom. At that time, South Africa still had the mandate to govern the country then known as South West Africa.

In 1968 Namibia landed a record catch – 1.4 million tonnes. Then began a typical "overkill" reaction from which the country never recovered. In 1969 the government, ignoring warnings of overfishing, increased the quota to 1.75 million tonnes. But only 1.2 million tonnes were caught, a big drop from the season before. A little perturbed by its miscalculation, the government reduced the 1970 quota to 810,000 tonnes. The catch fell even below that. Despite this, the world's biggest sardine cannery in Walvis Bay announced it was expanding its plant.

In 1971 the sardine catch dropped to its lowest level in years. The rape of this resource began to look deliberate. The quota in 1972 was almost 1 million tonnes – the catch was half of that. In 1973 the catch rose to almost 706,000 tonnes, leading to much figurative high-fiving in the Department of Agriculture and Fisheries. But the fishing industry was fatally misreading the situation. Under pressure, fish tend to compensate by rapid breeding; and a large percentage of the sardines caught were too young to have bred. What was happening was that anchovies, which have only a third of the nutritional value of sardines, had begun to fill the niche previously occupied by sardines; and much of the catch was anchovies. Unbelievably the government expanded Walvis Bay fishing harbour and, in 1977, again upped the quota to nearly a million tonnes. The catch barely reached 400,000 tonnes. Two fish factories closed.

In 1978 the sardine season was stopped halfway through. One thousand kilometres inland in Mpumalanga, South Africa's fruit-growing province, tomato farmers retrenched hundreds of workers; 80% of the tomatoes were for canned sardines, but the market had died. By 1980, only two fish factories remained open. The quota was down 99.2% on 10 years before – a mere 12,500 tonnes; even so, the trawlers came back with less than half. The anchovy, too, was in a steep decline.

By 1981 Namibia had closed its last fish factory, and 8,000 people became jobless. The trawlers were sold to Chile. Ever since, southern Africa has been forced to import canned sardines.

A lot of people behind the scenes grew rich from the rape of Namibia's coast. Many were closely connected to government, up to ministerial level.

In the same period, South Africa's own sardine shoals, from the Orange River mouth to Cape Agulhas in the south, were reduced by 95%. They too never recovered. West and East Germany, Russia, Britain, Norway, Belgium ... all helped plunder southern Africa's waters; each one knew that if it stopped, the others would carry on.

Africa's sardine crash was not unique; indeed, worse was happening off South America. In the late 1960s, Peru's anchovy fishing grounds were yielding 10 million tonnes a year. A US scientific commission warned that this catch rate was unsustainable. But the international fishing frenzy continued, and the following year the catch climbed to 12 million; then it crashed to nil.

The industry claimed that the failure was due to a natural fluctuation in the strength of the north-flowing Humboldt Current that normally caused huge upwellings of nutritious material for the fish. Yet even when the upwellings returned, the fish did not.

Under the Law of the Sea Convention, the territorial waters of a maritime nation extend 200 kilometres from the coast, and constitute an Exclusive Economic Zone for that nation. North of southern Africa's ravaged fishing grounds, there is a crescent of West African coastal countries that runs from Mauritania down to Sierra Leone, and borders an area of the Atlantic particularly rich in fish species. Day and night (using spotlights), fishing vessels with technologically advanced equipment fish there, in competition with West African fishermen operating from open boats (pirogues), sometimes 30 kilometres offshore. Some northern hemisphere countries pay the West African nations for permission to fish here; but the owners of the territorial waters have neither the equipment nor the funds to oversee them, so they have no control over how much is being caught off their shores. It's a matter of trust – and trust has never been a strong point among trawlermen.

In 2012, John Vidal of *The Guardian* described the scene in Mauritanian waters, from aboard Greenpeace's vessel the *Arctic Sunrise*:

"… within 50 miles of us are at least 20 of the biggest EU fishing vessels, along with Chinese, Russian and Icelandic trawlers and unidentifiable pirate ships.

"We are closest to the *Margaris*, a giant 9,499-tonne Lithuanian factory trawler able to catch, process and freeze 250 tonnes of fish a day, and a small Mauritanian vessel, the *Bab El Ishajr*. Here too, in the early mists, its radio identification signal switched off, is Spanish beam trawler the *Rojamar*. The *Arctic Sunrise*, Greenpeace's 40-year-old former ice-breaker, is shadowing one of Britain's biggest factory trawlers – the 4,957-tonne *Cornelis Vrolijk*. Operated by the North Atlantic Fishing Company (NAFC), based in Caterham, Surrey, it is one of 34 giant freezer vessels that regularly work the West African coast as part of the Pelagic Freezer Association (PFA), which represents nine European trawler owners.

"The ship, which employs Mauritanian fish processing workers aboard, is five miles away, heading due south at 13 knots out of dirty weather around Cape Blanc on the western Saharan border. By following the continental ledge in search of sardines, sardinella, and mackerel, it hopes to catch 3,000 tonnes of fish in a four- to six-week voyage before it offloads them, possibly in Las Palmas in the Canary Islands.

"But, says NAFC managing director Stewart Harper, while most of its fish will end up in Africa, none will go to Mauritania, despite the country facing a famine in parts."

(Vidal explains that Mauritania does not have the infrastructure to handle frozen fish or large vessels).

"The West African coast has some of the world's most abundant fishing grounds, but they are barely monitored or policed, and wide open to legal and illegal plunder. According to the UN's Food and Agriculture Organization, all West African fishing grounds are fully or overexploited, to the detriment of over 1.5 million local fishermen who cannot compete with (the fleets) or feed their growing populations.

"Heavily subsidised EU-registered fleets catch 235,000 tonnes of small pelagic species from Mauritanian and Moroccan waters alone a year, and tens of thousands of tonnes of other species in waters off Sierra Leone, Ghana, Guinea-Bissau and elsewhere.

"Despite possible ecological collapse, and growing evidence of declining catches in coastal waters, West African countries are now some of the EU's most-targeted fishing grounds, with 25% of all fish caught by its fleets coming from the waters of developing countries."

Vidal's *Guardian* report said about 50 international freezer-trawlers were active in Mauritanian waters at any one time, of which 30 originated from countries such as Russia, China, Korea and Belize.

The situation is unsustainable and immoral. Greenpeace told Vidal that it takes 56 traditional Mauritanian boats one year to catch the volume of fish that a PFA vessel can capture and process in a single day. In 2006 they found that over half of the 104 vessels observed off the coast of Guinea were either engaging in illegal fishing activities, or linked to them.

But the British-based PFA says banning EU vessels from African waters would not be sensible. Fish caught by the PFA goes to African communities, rather than consumers in developed countries. The PFA's catch, they say, is a major source of protein for the people in countries such as Nigeria.

The coastal belt

Mining and quarrying companies have been conscienceless transgressors in the coastal environment around Africa. De Beers, in its search for diamonds, used pressure hoses to blast sand as well as all sea life away from the recesses of the rocky shoreline of South Africa's West Coast, with its thousands of seals and other creatures. This made economic sense – but only to De Beers.

Over on the east coast, in 1990 the South African government gave the go-ahead for Richards Bay Minerals (RBM, part of Rio Tinto) to remove the high forested dunes that form the backdrop to Africa's biggest estuary, Lake St Lucia, which empties into the Indian Ocean. The dunes were rich in titanium, so that made economic sense too – to a very few. The titanium was for export to Canada – a country that had told the world it was boycotting apartheid South Africa in compliance with a United Nations resolution.

The estuary, with its fresh- and saltwater components, is a vast fish nursery with a complex ecology. In fact the iSimangaliso Wetland Park, which now incorporates the estuary, has eight different ecological zones and a wonderful biodiversity; it was at one time one of Africa's richest wildlife areas. The mine owners planned to remove the dunes down to bedrock and pump the sand through a massive floating factory to extract the titanium, operating 24 hours a day and using arc lights at night. They promised to reconstruct each dune 500 metres further along the coast, and replant the indigenous forest.

I interviewed the Minister of Environment who had sanctioned the mining and realised he was hopelessly under the sway of the mining company. So were the country's biggest conservation groups, the Endangered Wildlife Trust (I am one of its three founders) and the Wildlife Society, whose president also happened to be president of the Chamber of Mines. Both institutions were receiving major funding from the mining company.

The minister displayed no environmental understanding or concern whatever – just a breathtaking cynicism. During the interview he announced, totally out of the blue, that St Lucia would be made a game reserve – even though the mine would be operating at its central and highest point, and special roads were to be made for the trucks.

The public, with much support from the media and from conservation-aware countries such as Germany, protested vigorously: 1990 was a good time to campaign. There was optimism in the air; the Soviet Union had collapsed, the Berlin Wall had just come down, Nelson Mandela was released after almost 30 years in prison, and apartheid was about to end. The African National Congress, now unbanned and soon to win a general election, clearly had a different view of environmental matters, and rejected the mining. The apartheid-era minister disappeared into obscurity.

Today the much-abused estuary, after being used as a missile and artillery testing ground, drilled for oil, planted with 14,000 hectares of alien pine trees, and having its freshwater supply blocked by ill-advised hydrological developments, is a huge and tranquil game reserve – one of the most exciting wetlands in Africa. Few thought the region would recover, but the iSimangaliso Wetland Park is once more teeming with wildlife, much of which seemed to come out of hiding after the pine plantation was removed.

The park today extends 230 kilometres up to the Mozambique border and incorporates the entire estuary as well as South Africa's largest freshwater lake – Lake Sibaya – and even more estuarine lakes in the north and coral reefs offshore. I recently revisited the park; at a spot where 20 years ago I had driven along a track hemmed in by alien pines, I could now see the long line of naturally forested dunes along the eastern shore. On either side of the road, buffalo grazed in the long grass; a female white rhino and her calf held us up for a while. Andrew Zaloumis, the park's CEO, said, "Africa recovers very quickly, given the chance. RBM promised mining would create 600 jobs, or was it 300? I've forgotten. The park employs, directly, 3,000 and often needs additional labour."

On the other side of the dunes the park administers a 250-kilometre-long, unsullied golden beach where, at night, turtles weighing up to a tonne plough a shallow furrow as they drag themselves up the sand to lay their eggs beneath the dunes.

Shellfish

South African crayfish (rock lobster), once common, are now greatly reduced in quantity and in average size. They have become far too expensive for the average South African to buy; yet not many years ago they were part of the staple diet of poor people living along the coast. Now those same people are heavily fined or jailed if they are found in possession of crayfish without a permit. The quaint fishermen's cottages have now been converted to accommodate tourists, but the restaurants no longer offer crayfish.

Some years ago, the South African Police Services impounded 21 trawlers carrying 750 tonnes of crayfish – 10 times their collective quota.

California, having learned the hard way about overutilising coastal resources (think of Steinbeck's *Cannery Row*), no longer exports its shellfish. If you want to enjoy it, you have to go there. As a consequence its lobsters and crabs are cheaper and far superior in size and quality to those found in Africa.

Another shellfish that has become too expensive for the locals is perlemoen or abalone, *Haliotis midae* – a large and tasty mollusc found only in South Africa. According to a fisheries conference in 2016 it is now being poached – nearly all for the Far Eastern market – at an unsustainable level. South Africa reinstated its abalone fishing industry a few years ago but government figures show the illegal offtake is 10 times bigger that the legal. The 2016 conference heard that in the previous year, poachers stole 7 million abalone – almost double the 2008 figure. Illegally obtained perlemoen are mostly sold to Japan, China and Vietnam where they are an expensive delicacy and believed to have aphrodisiacal powers. Two men, arrested in Namibia in 2016 for possessing poached rhino horn, were also in possession of hundreds of dried perlemoen from the Cape. The shellfish were worth more than the horns.

Sharks

There is growing concern regarding the worldwide decline in shark numbers. Of the 400 species that exist, one-third are considered threatened, according to the IUCN. Several species are being fished off Africa; and the biggest and one of the most ubiquitous, the great white shark, once so common off Africa's coastline, is now threatened with extinction. Stellenbosch University marine biologist Sara Andreotti, who found that the trailing edges of the dorsal fins can be used to identify individual sharks, spent seven years researching their numbers off the South African coast. In 2017 she found that the number of great white sharks did not exceed 522 and might even be as low as 353 – 5% lower than previously calculated.

According to a 2009 report by the IUCN's Shark Specialist Group, just over half the sharks then being fished were killed by fishing vessels specialising in deep-sea tuna and swordfish. Sharks were considered a by-catch; but as the demand for shark fin soup grew – driven by the new stratum of wealthy Chinese and Vietnamese – so prices soared and "finning" became a problem. Finning is the practice of cutting off a shark's fins and dumping the rest over the side. The practice was outlawed, under CITES, in 2013 but surveillance is almost impossible.

A study released in March 2013 by researchers at Dalhousie University in Halifax, Canada, and published in the peer-reviewed journal *Marine Policy*, said 100 million sharks are killed each year in commercial fisheries – a rate of fishing that is unsustainable. WildAid, a US-based organisation focusing on reducing demand for wildlife products, estimates that of the 100 million, up to 73 million are killed only for their fins, which are bound for China, Vietnam and Japan.

Shark fin soup, a centuries-old tradition at weddings and banquets in the Far East, owes its chewy texture to the fin and its flavour to other ingredients. Nevertheless, a bowl of shark fin soup can cost $1,000 and the fin of a basking shark currently sells for $10,000.

But as we have seen elsewhere, China, by far the world's biggest consumer of shark fin soup, has been steering towards the conservation of the world's beleaguered wildlife resources. Among the reform policies it announced towards the end of 2016 was a proposed ban on shark fin imports. It had by then already stopped serving shark fin soup and bird's-nest soup at state functions, and launched an effective poster campaign asking people to stop eating soup made from wild animal parts. According to a report by WildAid, shark fin consumption in China fell by 50–70% between 2011 and 2013; sales of shark fin in Guangzhou, considered to be the centre of the shark fin trade in China, dropped by 82%.

Gerald Durrell offered the best advice, though he was talking about turtle soup:

"If your host offers you (shark fin) soup, decline it. If he persists, pour it on his carpet."

Whales

The marine megafauna around Africa comprises some startling species, including the largest creature that ever lived, the blue whale. Nobody is sure how it survived the Pleistocene, which saw several ice ages and global warming episodes leading to radical changes in the oceans, both in depth and in temperature.

But this creature is now seen more and more off the African coast. It eats 3 tonnes of tiny shrimp-like krill every day, and gives birth to a calf that weighs 2 tonnes and probably drinks about 1,000 litres of milk daily.

The 20th century's turnabout in whale populations proves that when the chips are down, the world can rally to a cause. According to the International Whaling Commission (IWC), formed just in time (in 1946) to protect the future of whales, the blue whale's global population was reduced by more than 99% during the 20th century – the result of conscienceless hunting. A count of the species in the Antarctic, its favourite region, showed it was down to 360 individuals – about 0.15% of its original numbers.

The blue whale, found in every corner of every ocean, had been hunted since the 1600s, first by the Dutch and then the English who maintained large fleets. It was by far the most mercilessly hunted creature in the sea. As whale numbers fell in the more temperate waters, so the hunt began in the south polar seas. By the 1800s the Americans had moved in, and factory ships were developed. The ships became faster, the techniques more streamlined. By the mid-1800s the whalers, no longer restricted to hunting the slower whales such as humpback and sperm whales from open boats, could now chase the faster, sleeker and far less barnacle-encrusted blue whale. The killing became more frenzied and explosive-headed missiles were used, which might as well have been classed as naval ordnance.

A fully grown whale, within an hour of being harpooned and winched aboard a factory ship, would be flensed – using long, two-handed, razor-sharp knives – and the heavy strips of blubber fed into boilers to produce 25 to 30 tonnes of edible oil. The oil's value was immense, for it was used for lamps, candles, soap, lubricants and cosmetics. It was also processed into cooking oil and margarine. The bones became corsets, umbrella ribs and bone meal. The meat, because of the krill intake, was like thick, tender but rather fishy-tasting beef. The tendons became "cat gut" for tennis rackets.

In 1859 there was a reprieve, as the world's first oil derricks began to sprout; petroleum quickly replaced whale oil as fuel. In spite of this, in the first third of the 20th century whale numbers plummeted to an unprecedented low, and extinction loomed for some species.

The humpback whale, once the most common species off Africa's east coast, all but disappeared; and the southern right whale, once so prolific in the spring along the coastline of southern Africa, was in those days rarely seen in its favourite breeding grounds such as the Western Cape's False Bay. The plummeting numbers became alarming; if alternative oil sources had not been found, some whale species might well have been hunted to extinction.

In 1946, the IWC temporarily banned commercial whaling and in 1986 agreed upon an "indefinite moratorium". Norway demurred and so did Japan, though the latter claimed to confine itself to hunting for "research purposes" – a brazen subterfuge, for its restaurants are never short of whale delicacies.

The blue whale in the southern waters is recovering well, at a rate of about 7.3% a year according to the IWC, but it remains well below its pre-whaling numbers. The IUCN estimates there are 10,000 to 25,000 blue whales worldwide, in five separate populations.

In springtime, people living in the Cape around False Bay and Hermanus are once again being wakened at dawn by the sound of the 40-tonne southern right whales mating in the surf. Tourists are annually paying millions to come to Africa to take part in "whale watching". They watch mostly southern rights and humpbacks, from a respectful distance. The whales usually don't seem to mind, though a humpback off the Cape that thought a yacht was coming too close (and possibly worried about its calf) launched itself out of the sea and landed, all 40 tonnes of it, on the yacht. It did tremendous damage but fortunately the sailors were unharmed.

With increased shipping, whales are sometimes killed in collisions and some are washed up fatally entangled in nets. It is believed that ever-increasing artificial ocean noise, including sonar, interferes with the low-frequency vocalisations of whales, which they use to communicate across hundreds of miles of water. A further threat to their future is the tonnage of PCB (polychlorinated biphenyl) plastic floating in the oceans, which some species, feeding by taking vast quantities of krill-filled water into their enormous mouths, inevitably swallow.

Dolphins

Dolphins are miniature (toothed) whales of the family Delphinidae, with horizontally flattened tails or flukes. The biggest of the dolphins is the killer whale or orca, whose male has a huge characteristic dorsal fin. It is a most handsome creature, with a glossy black skin and striking white marking. Orcas hunt in packs along the coast of Africa and, from Cape Point rocks, I once watched three chasing some smaller dolphins at motor-torpedo boat speed. The species status is healthy.

The most-seen dolphin off the African coast is the bottle-nosed, *Tursiops aduncus*, which hunts shoals in large groups. I have seen 150, perhaps more, herding a shoal of fish into Hout Bay, but the average group off KwaZulu-Natal, where they are seen daily, is around 20. The population is healthy though as with so many other dolphin species, individuals drown after getting ensnared in shark nets off KwaZulu-Natal, and many more die caught up in fishermen's nets. They are also susceptible to estuarine pollution.

The common, or long-beaked dolphin, *Delphinus capensis*, is found all around Africa and indeed across all the oceans, though the species around Africa has been deemed a separate one. They are found in groups numbering between 500 and 3,000. Ocean Africa, which says over 9,000 were sighted off Plettenberg Bay in 1999, describes them as "very gregarious and (they) positively 'love' boats. Moving at high speeds while chasing prey, they will utilise the bow wave and the wake of a boat to save energy." I've seen them criss-crossing ahead of the bows of an ocean liner just before the entrance to Durban Harbour.

Dugongs

Less robust than the dolphins are the walrus-like dugongs that graze the seagrass along the coastlines of the western Indian

Ocean; a diminishing few are found in the warm water off East Africa. *Dugong dugon* belongs to the order Sirenia, whose euphonious name is based on the Greek myth of the Sirens – beautiful island women who enticed the crews of passing ships to come closer to shore, and then watched gleefully as they wrecked their boats on the rocks. Sailors, seeing the pale-skinned dugongs, fancied they were sirens; maybe the sun was in their eyes, or maybe they'd been at sea longer than was healthy.

Dugongs, which once were numerous, have been reduced to isolated herds, and in Africa are down to around 500; a few occur in Mozambique's Bazaruto Archipelago, which is as far south as they get.

Their population is wholly dependent on seagrass and has been in a steady decline since the 1960s because of habitat destruction, pollution and the scarcity of food in hard times. The dugong has become extinct around Mauritius and Rodrigues Island, and is classed as "vulnerable".

Manatees

The herbivorous manatee or sea cow is another species in the order Sirenia found in Africa. It is so slow-moving as it swims just below the sea's surface that algae grows on its back and might even act as a sun block. It has an egg-shaped head, flippers and a flat dolphin-like tail. The 500 kilogram African manatee, *Trichechus senegalensis*, occurs in West African coastal waters from Mauritania down to Angola. It has been recorded 10 kilometres out to sea, and 2,000 kilometres up the Niger River.

After years of losing habitats due to development, and being hunted and ensnared in fishing nets, it is probably down to 10,000 individuals and has disappeared from many of its former haunts. It is classified as "vulnerable" in the IUCN's Red List.

Seals

The African coast has only one resident pinniped – the Cape fur seal, *Arctocephalus pusillus*. It is the largest of the world's fur seals and is found all around the southern African coast, from Port Elizabeth in the east to almost as far north as Angola in the west.

Strictly speaking it is not a seal. True seals have no ear flaps and a single rear flipper, and generally drag themselves along on their stomachs. Cape fur seals, like the sea lions to which they are related, have two distinct rear "feet" in the shape of flippers and are thus able to walk, or rather waddle, on all fours. They are covered in dense brown hair, and the males may weigh up to 350 kilograms.

The IUCN regards the species as safe, and has assigned them to the "least concern" category on the Red List. In 2010 there were an estimated 1.5 to 2 million, of which two-thirds were in Namibia.

Soon after the females give birth, Namibia holds an annual cull, sometimes accounting for as many as 85,000 pups and 2,000 bulls. The pups are clubbed on the head (this is deemed to be the most merciful way to kill them) and are harvested for their fur. Fortunately the seal-fur trade is dying. But a new market has sprung up: bulls are being harvested for their genitals, to feed Vietnam and China's aphrodisiac trade. According to a *Cape Argus* report, the sale of seal genitalia is today the most lucrative part of the industry.

A shop in Cape Town, specialising in Chinese goods, was found illegally selling "seal kits" comprising a dried penis and testicles, for R10,000 each.

The Namibian government claims culling is necessary because the seals are competing with its commercial fish catch; but it has produced no scientific evidence to support this, and it has also been claimed that mathematical modelling studies disprove it. The complexity of the marine food web is such that some authorities claim seal culling might actually reduce the commercial catch of other staples of the human diet, such as hake.

Namibia is planning a factory complex at Henties Bay which will incorporate a seal abattoir, bone meal plant, fat-processing plant (with laboratories for the bottling and manufacturing of oils, capsules, creams and cosmetics), tannery, shoe factory, leatherware factory, canning factory, research laboratory, museum and retail sales outlet.

In South Africa, fur seals have been protected in one way or another since 1893. The most recent legislation is the Sea Birds and Seals Protection Act of 1973, which affords complete protection, but allows the government to grant permits to kill fur seals at specific colonies. Between 1973 and 1982, permits were granted for killing an annual average of 18,750 pups and 530 adult males. From 1983 to 1990 the numbers fluctuated around an annual average of 3,500 pups and 4,300 bulls. Following many public protests, the annual cull was abandoned in 1990.

8 The game is on

We fully recognise that our game
reserves belong to the world and not just
to us. We agree they are part of the world's
natural heritage and that we have a
responsibility to look after them. But as
our reserves are part of the world's heritage
then the world must help pay for them
because we can't afford it.

Zulu politician, Chief Mangosuthu Buthelezi

In sub-Saharan Africa, the years 2015 and 2016 were the worst of years and the best of years. They will go down in conservation history as the costliest in terms of the wanton slaughter of Africa's megafauna. They will also go down as the turn of the tide.

Africa had been suffering an invasion, led mainly by the Chinese whose government turned a blind eye to its criminal syndicates as they established supply chains to smuggle wild animal parts from Africa. The Chinese were joined by wild animal traffickers from Vietnam, Malaysia, the Philippines, Laos, Thailand and Japan.

In Africa, as the destruction of its megafauna peaked, it became obvious that China's future actions would decide if Africa's elephant, lion and other species were to survive. African poachers could not resist the fees the syndicates were paying, and the syndicates had bribed officials and politicians; in some cases, even the head of state was in on the deal.

THE GAME IS ON | 167

The period climaxed with elephant and lion populations crashing to unprecedented lows. In a matter of months, well over 1,000 rhino were slaughtered.

Over the last few years, hundreds of Chinese and Vietnamese nationals – expatriates living in Africa as well as visitors and even diplomats – have been implicated in the casual slaughter of protected species. Their incursions have cost, annually, not only the deaths of tens of thousands of elephants, rhinoceroses, lions, and other terrestrial and marine animals, but also the deaths of hundreds of game rangers and security forces, not to mention a great many of the poachers themselves, recruited from impecunious villages and paid extravagant rewards.

Every country south of the Sahara has been pillaged. In the last few years, 90% of the contraband has gone to China and Vietnam, with their governments' full knowledge. The cost to Africa has been enormous.

A letter handed over to the Chinese ambassador to Namibia, Xin Shunkang, on 16 December 2016, epitomised the situation. Namibia's economy is strongly dependent on eco-tourism, and it pursues an exemplary, community-sensitive wildlife conservation policy. The Chinese onslaught had become so unendurable that it caused 40 of Namibia's conservation and natural science institutions to appeal to the ambassador to act – urgently. The letter, delivered to the embassy by the Namibian Chamber of Environment, will have resonated with conservationists throughout the African subcontinent.

I have had to shorten it:

"Dear Ambassador Xin Shunkang,

"During the past few weeks, several Chinese nationals have been apprehended and charged with wildlife crimes, including illegal possession of rhino horn, ivory and pangolin skins and scales.

"Your embassy is on record stating that 'it will not allow a few of its nationals who have been arrested in connection with poaching to tarnish its country's image'.

"While we recognise that not all Chinese nationals are involved in wildlife crimes, Namibia's environmental community believes that the situation ... is far more serious and broad-based than you have acknowledged. ... you and your country are best placed to address the problem.

"Until the arrival of Chinese nationals in significant numbers in Namibia, commercial wildlife crime was extremely low. As Chinese nationals moved into all regions of Namibia, setting up businesses, networks, acquiring mineral prospecting licences and offering payment for wildlife products, the incidence of poaching, illegal wildlife capture, collection, killing and export has increased exponentially. Chinese nationals have been involved in, and/or are the commercial drivers behind:

1. the escalating poaching of rhinos and elephants in Namibia and the illegal export of rhino horn and ivory,
2. the capture, trade and export of pangolins,
3. the import of Chinese monofilament nets in industrial quantities via Zambia to the northeast of Namibia, which are destroying the fisheries of the Zambezi, Chobe, Kwando and Okavango rivers,
4. the unsustainable commercialisation of fisheries in these northeastern rivers and wetland systems for export to cities and towns in neighbouring countries,
5. the capture and killing of carmine bee-eaters at their breeding colonies by means of nets,
6. the rise in bushmeat poaching wherever Chinese nationals are working on road construction and other infrastructure, including tortoises, monitor lizards, pythons and any other form of wild meat, including from protected and endangered species,

7. the illegal collection of shellfish on the Namibian coast,
8. the illegal transit through Namibia and attempted export of poached abalone from Cape waters through Namibian ports.

"We are also aware of long-standing interests by some Chinese nationals to start a shark fin industry in Namibia, a practice that has caused widespread damage to shark populations in many parts of the world, including in South Africa.

"More recently, Chinese nationals have proposed to capture marine mammals and seabirds.

"We are concerned by an apparent total disregard by some Chinese nationals for Namibia's wildlife, conservation, and animal welfare laws and values.

"Namibians are proud of their environmental heritage ... and (have) worked hard to protect and nurture these natural assets. Namibia's wildlife management provides an international example for good conservation and sustainable use.

"The illegal commercial interests of some Chinese nationals towards Namibia's protected wildlife has exploited the vulnerability of poor Namibians and divided societies. It undermines local ownership of natural resources and the empowerment of communities to manage their wildlife wisely, for long-term communal benefits. It undermines Namibia's globally acclaimed Community-based Conservancy programme, and it does considerable damage to Namibia's international conservation and sustainable development reputation.

"The recent announcement by the Chinese business community that it is contributing N$30,000 to counter rhino poaching ... is an insult. *(One Namibian dollar is equivalent to one South African Rand)*. An initial, very conservative estimate of the extent of the losses to Namibia's wildlife and ecosystems caused by Chinese nationals is about N$811 million. This does not include the significant additional resources that Namibia's government, donors, communities, private sector, and NGOs have had to commit to combat escalating wildlife crimes ...

"We do not claim to fully understand the relationship between Chinese nationals and the Chinese state. It appears that Chinese nationals are not at liberty to obtain passports and travel independently around the world, bringing their personal capital and starting businesses in their own names ... Chinese nationals in Namibia appear to be part of a state-supported system. So, as the highest ranking Chinese official in Namibia ... we now call on you to put an immediate stop to the illegal wildlife crimes perpetrated, encouraged, funded, incentivised or otherwise committed and supported by some Chinese nationals in Namibia. Further, we call on the Chinese government to make good, by investing in Namibia's environment sector in a transparent and internationally recognised manner, and in proportion to the damage caused, to help rebuild Namibia's wildlife populations, ecosystems, management systems and reputation.

"This letter does not represent only the views of the 40 environmental organisations listed below, but also represents the views of countless members of the Namibian public and our international friends. The sentiments expressed in social media over the past months, from across a broad spectrum of Namibian society, and their outrage at the leading role that Chinese nationals play in wildlife crime, have surely been noted by you and members of your embassy. You will also be aware of the sentiments expressed by our President, by the Minister of Environment and Tourism, and by the Namibian Police Inspector General as reported in the local media.

"China has a policy of non-intervention and yet these actions ... and the apparent inaction of your embassy to address the problem, are direct and indirect interventions that have disastrous impacts on our policy and legal framework, on our environmental culture and ethics, on our natural heritage and on our national conservation and development programmes. They also have huge negative impacts on our people and their livelihoods, and on our international reputation.

"In the last couple of years, particularly under the leadership of your President Xi Jinping, China has taken a decidedly more active leadership role in global issues. It is time to extend that leadership to natural resources and, in particular, to wildlife conservation ... We counter all forms of xenophobia and profiling. However, we expect foreign investors and their nationals to abide by Namibia's laws, and to embrace Namibia's cultures, ethics, and values. Too many Chinese nationals have abused Namibia's environmental laws, and this is causing growing resentment.

"We are also concerned at how little action the Chinese embassy in Namibia appears to be taking to address the problem.

"We, as concerned Namibian Environmental NGOs and businesses ... stand ready to work with a China that willingly takes on greater responsibility and leadership in addressing the illegal trade in wildlife and commits to putting an immediate stop to all wildlife crimes in Namibia by its nationals."

The letter was signed by Dr Chris Brown, CEO, Namibian Chamber of Environment.

Coincidentally (perhaps), it was less than a fortnight after the Namibian letter – in fact on New Year's Day 2017 – that China made its dramatic announcement about the end of ivory sales, as described in Chapter Five. Vietnam was also showing signs of curbing the trade. In March 2017 Vietnam's state-controlled media reported that 100 kilograms of rhino horn in two suitcases coming from Kenya had been confiscated at Hanoi Airport. No arrests were mentioned. Hanoi had still not announced any intention of complying with the CITES proposals for stronger measures against illegal wildlife imports.

It seems possible that before 2020, the Far East will have quit plundering Africa; but after any war, the aggressor is obliged to pay reparations. China and Vietnam, if held to account as they must be, should be forced to help fund the restoration of the areas they have allowed to be ravaged and the species they have plundered.

A day after the Chinese announcement on ivory sales, Shanghai customs officers arrested two people trying to import 3 tonnes of African pangolin (scaly anteater) scales. Such a quantity would have entailed the killing of between 5,000 and 7,500 "protected" pangolins – a small proportion of the estimated annual 100,000 tonnes that are being illegally transported from Africa for the Chinese market. The powdered-down scales are thought to have medicinal powers comparable to those of rhino horn; but being of the same material (keratin), they have no such powers. Pangolin flesh is also regarded as a delicacy; the Far East ate its own pangolins into near oblivion years ago, and the poachers of Chinese pangolins receive long sentences – hence the traders' interest in the African variety.

Habitat poaching

Julie Clarke-Havemann, an environmental analyst and specialist on land use policies with the Development Bank of Southern Africa, warns that it is not just animals, but entire habitats that are being poached. She describes the trucks one sees on Mozambican roads, laden with the trunks of giant tropical forest trees – all bound for China. The trade, though illegal, has been going on for years.

A 2014 Greenpeace report stated that illegal deforestation was happening across tropical Africa as well as Madagascar. "Complete deforestation of the African Congo Basin", according to the report, "is predicted to intensify the West African monsoon, while increasing temperatures and (halving) rainfall in the entire region". In Namibia's Caprivi Strip (now known as the Zambezi Region) truckloads of kiaat (the tree produces a rich red wood) are being hauled out for shipment to China. No environmental impact assessment has been made public.

From 2015 onwards it became increasingly evident that the Far East, particularly China, was beginning to realise it had to distance itself from the looming wildlife disaster into which it had plunged Africa. What remains to be seen, in 2017 and beyond, is how vigilant its customs officials are going to be at China's ports of entry, and how the penalties will be adjusted to fit the crimes. Bear in mind that China can impose a life sentence on anybody who poaches China's own iconic species, the panda.

The ecological culture gap

There is the perception across sub-Saharan Africa that the formal conservation of wildlife and protected areas is a white idiosyncrasy – which it certainly was until well into the 20th century. Initially, neither black communities nor white colonials were particularly concerned about conservation or ecological sustainability. To many of the colonials, wildlife was a commodity to be traded; to Africans it was *nyama*, to be eaten. It was always abundant until the population grew and hunting became rapacious. Very few people, until the dawn of the 20th century, saw the wonder of African wildlife, or saw it as a tourist attraction or a sustainable food resource. Then came the proliferation of game reserves; the *nyama* was fenced in and those who'd traditionally lived off it were fenced out. The reserves' visitors were mainly car-owning whites.

The former colonial powers laid the foundations for rural Africa's indifference towards wildlife. Once the authorities began to realise the value of wildlife, and the moral obligation to preserve it for future humans, they imposed laws against Africans, instead of with them. In many regions, they displaced rural dwellers to make way for animals. But in so doing, they had devalued wildlife in the eyes of those who dwelt in the wilds, of those who are the de facto primary custodians of wildlife.

In a challenging 1967 article in *Science* magazine, titled *The Historical Roots of Our Ecological Crisis*, Lynn White Jnr wrote of how the Judaeo-Christian tradition, by taking the Bible so literally, saw the Book of Genesis as giving humanity an open hunting licence. Did it not say we must "subdue" the Earth and "have dominion over all the fish of the sea, and over the fowl of the air, and over every living thing"? Too late, the church authorities changed the biblical translation from reading "dominion" to "stewardship". But the missionaries had already done their work as they saw it, which was to crush, in schools and in places of worship, the original respect for nature, and replace it with the view that nature was there purely for the benefit of humans.

White wrote: "In antiquity, every tree, every spring, every stream, every hill had its own *genius loci*, its guardian spirit. These spirits were accessible to men, but were very unlike men ... Before one cut a tree, mined a mountain, or dammed a brook, it was important to placate the spirit in charge of that particular institution, and to keep it placated. By destroying pagan animism, Christianity made it possible to exploit nature in a mood of indifference."

The survival of the megafauna

I said at the beginning of this book that I held an optimistic view. I am encouraged by the steadily growing number of heavily-attended global, regional and pan-African conferences and their increasingly practical plenary sessions, all focusing on making our peace with the natural world and maintaining biodiversity. Biodiversity is little understood, yet it is as important as the air we breathe. Maintaining global biodiversity is the new universal *oriflamme* and Africa, when it comes to biodiversity, happens to be the richest region on Earth.

Africa's living organisms comprise around a quarter of global biodiversity and include the Earth's greatest assemblages of large mammals. Its biomes extend from mangrove swamps to deserts, from balmy Mediterranean coastlines to tropical forests, from montane ecosystems to grassy plains.

Its threats include massive and mindless population growth, poor resource management, rampant corruption, unplanned urbanisation, rich and poor living beyond their environmental income, and massive destruction caused by alien invasive plants smothering natural Africa.

Despite all this, Africa has preserved, against almost overwhelming odds, the Earth's largest intact populations of large mammals. During the recent overkill period – let's say the last 200 years – sub-Saharan Africa has lost only two species of megafauna, both unique to South Africa. The blue buck, *Hippotragus leucophaeus*, related to the sable, became extinct in 1799 or 1800, and the last known quagga, *Equus quagga*, died in 1883 in Amsterdam Zoo. The last known wild Cape lion, actually a subspecies, *Panthera leo melanochaitus*, was shot near Colesberg in 1838; but most of the lions in Eurasian circuses and menageries originated from the Cape, and so this subspecies may yet be capable of resuscitation.

Sadly, many of Africa's creatures are now vulnerable to extinction according to the IUCN's Red Data List, and one or two have even been downgraded to the "critically endangered" category. The cheetah, for instance, which once roamed throughout Africa as far afield as India, is now confined to 2% of its historic range. About a third of Africa's last 7,500 cheetahs survive in Namibia, where they may still be legally hunted under tight regulations.

Even the gentle giraffe is now considered vulnerable to extinction. In 1985 the IUCN believed there were about 163,000 giraffe. By the year 2000 they were below 100,000. Now they may number not much over 80,000.

It was once believed that all giraffe belonged to one species and so, at a population of 100,000 or more, they seemed to be borderline safe. In fact, giraffe are divided into four species. The common giraffe, *Giraffa camelopardalis*, is found from Zululand's iSimangaliso Wetland Park (St Lucia) all the way up to East Africa. There's an isolated subspecies in West Africa, known as the Nigerian giraffe, which is down to its last 300 members, though some sources say there may be only 100. In 1990, East Africa had about 27,000 giraffe in three distinct species. Now they are down to as few as 3,000.

A major cause of the giraffe's decline is human population growth and the resultant conflict over space. Poaching became a factor when it was rumoured that their brains and bone marrow could cure HIV/AIDS, even though there's no foundation to this. Nevertheless, poachers can get $140 (almost R2,000) for a freshly severed giraffe head or bones; and like most wild animals, whether it's Cecil the lion or a 7-tonne tusker, a giraffe is so easy to kill these days.

Of the "Big Five" – the five species of megafauna considered by hunters to be the most dangerous to hunt (because they can fight back) – the wild lion is probably now the most vulnerable, followed by the elephant and the rhino. The remaining two are the leopard and the Cape buffalo. The latter is widespread, and possibly numbers around 1 million in its natural range across sub-Saharan Africa.

The leopard is the most beautiful of Africa's megafauna. Like Britain's foxes, the southern African leopard is capable of surviving near a metropolis and may even enter suburbia at night. In 2016 the species was listed as "vulnerable" – just one category short of "endangered", but this is mainly because of its decline in Asia, where several subspecies exist. The African leopard, *Panthera pardus*, has been reduced in numbers by habitat loss, trophy hunting, and the demand for its skin in tribal regalia; fortunately, in the western world, leopard-skin coats are no longer fashionable. In southern Africa the leopard is still widely though thinly distributed.

Biodiversity

Many years ago a story was reported that illustrates the fragility of biodiversity. Farmers in the Western Cape's wheat belt had mounted a campaign to get rid of snakes and, in the process, killed off mole snakes on a large scale. Mole snakes, which are non-venomous, live off rodents. Thus the rodents, especially gerbils, began to multiply and threatened the grain harvest. So the farmers put out poison. Within a short time, scavenging seagulls were dropping from the sky; they'd been eating dead gerbils. This, in turn, was said to account for an increased proportion of diseased fish caught by trawlers – the depleted seagulls could no longer keep the shoals healthy by preying on the sick stragglers.

I have not managed to find a scientific paper to confirm this report, which I recall from the 1980s; but it does illustrate – even if only in parable form – how everything is interconnected in this planet's bewilderingly complex web of biodiversity.

The importance of biodiversity is manifest in the Amazon jungle. The forest has existed for tens of millions of years on a surprisingly thin layer of soil – yet it is the planet's most stable ecosystem. Its area, 5.5 million square kilometres, is about equal to that of the lower third of Africa. The Amazon alone may have as many as 20 million species of living things, mostly invertebrates; every creature has a role. By analogy with the Amazon, one can assume that the forests of Central Africa also have many millions of species.

Variety is not just the spice of life, but its very essence. The fundamental need of any healthy ecosystem is species diversity. The areas with the least biodiversity and the lowest productivity are, of course, deserts, which produce almost nothing. By contrast a rain forest can produce, annually, something like 1,100 tonnes of growth per hectare. Remove the forest, and in its place, plant grain; the only surviving creatures will be those that eat grain – the antithesis of biodiversity. A grain failure would cause the collapse of everything.

A single example can serve to illustrate the interdependence of species in the rain forest. During long periods when the rainfall is low, succulent species of trees, being less susceptible to drought, thrust through the canopy of the receding deciduous trees, shading the latter from the sun. When the rains resume, the heavily water-dependent broad-leaf trees shoot up and protect the more succulent species – thus there is a dynamic equilibrium, and when death overtakes any living creature or plant, it dutifully returns its nitrogen to the common pool.

Ultimately, saving Africa's wildlife will require sustaining Africa's ecosystems and habitats, now under threat from many angles. Guy Preston, who heads the Environmental Programme in the South African Department of Environmental Affairs, argues that human-induced biological invasions will have the single greatest impact on biodiversity in the future. The World Conservation Union agrees it is a major problem but believes habitat loss is more important – but then much habitat loss is because of alien vegetation.

Invasive alien species, says Preston, become predators, competitors, parasites, and hybridisers of native plants, and have reduced the nutritional value of massive areas of Africa.

International awareness

One of many recent and positive strides made by the international community was a unanimously accepted global strategic plan for maintaining biodiversity, adopted in 2010 by the parties to the Convention on Biological Diversity (CBD) at a meeting in Nagoya, capital city of the Aichi Prefecture in Japan. The *Strategic Plan for Biodiversity 2011–2020* sets out a 10-year framework "for action by all countries and stakeholders to conserve biodiversity and enhance its benefits for people". It stems from a shared vision, a mission, and sets out strategic goals – 20 ambitious yet achievable targets, collectively known as the Aichi Biodiversity Targets. Some targets have already been reached, some may not be reached by 2020, but the treaty is indicative of the way global thinking is going.

Another recent sign of widespread concern for the planet's plants and animals is the number of very heavily attended international conferences focusing on the global environment; Africa's scientists and environmentally concerned officials have been increasingly active in these events. The last few years have witnessed many major conferences, often inspired by the United Nations but also initiated by the international scientific community, calling for focused meetings of the world's minds. The "talk festivals" of the past have given way to concrete proposals and plans on issues such as the alarming anthropogenic changes to the world's atmosphere; overfishing; global deforestation; hazardous substances; alien invasives; freshwater supply; desertification, and so on.

It was, I suppose, the United Nations Convention on the Law of the Sea (UNCLOS, concluded in 1982) that first demonstrated how, when the chips are down, even the most belligerent and difficult of nations can find common purpose in caring for the planet's life support system – the biosphere. The nations had first got together in 1958, in the hope of reaching agreement regarding the use of 71% of the Earth's surface – the oceans. That era marked the height of international silliness, when East and West (read communist and capitalist) were at loggerheads, and neither political system had an environmental history of which it could be proud. UNCLOS achieved international agreement regarding the rights and responsibilities of nations when using the world's oceans.

In the 1990s the Convention on Climate Change – calling for a reduction of greenhouse-gas emissions – was adopted unanimously, and it came into force in 2005. It proved to be inadequate. Yet it was universally agreed that if the atmosphere was to be restored to what it was before the Industrial Revolution, strict and binding guidelines were essential – despite industrialists' protests.

The conferences, workshops and seminars came in quick succession, each one sharper in focus than the last, until, at the end of 2016, at Le Bourget in France, thousands of representatives from 195 nations – that's almost every nation on Earth – stood and applauded when the gavel came down on the "Paris Accord". The agreement was reached to commit the world's leading economies to accepting mandatory targets on greenhouse-gas emissions and so help stave off the more drastic effects of climate change. The USA later reneged on the deal but most countries felt duty bound to continue.

In mid-2017 the International Energy Agency (IEA) reported that since 2013, carbon emissions had dropped below the levels recorded in America and Britain in the early

1990s. It found that energy-related carbon dioxide emissions had levelled off for a third year in a row, despite the global Gross Domestic Product (GDP) having risen 3.1%. A global Norwegian project in 2016 indicated targets may be less painful than initially feared.

The African renaissance

An essential step in the process of healing natural Africa will be to overcome the tribal divisions that have tended to overwhelm any holistic national and, ultimately, pan-African environmental goals. The only unifying element within some African countries seems to be their national soccer team. But, with slowly improving education, this too is changing.

As described in the preceding chapters, there are many cross-border plans to fuse protected areas.

Once Africa has been liberated from the neo-colonial forces presently invading it – as the Far Eastern exploiters start to relinquish their grip and leave Africa's wildlife alone – the renaissance of the world's greatest biodiversified region can begin and the gentle, sustainable, world-captivating industry of eco-tourism can expand. Southern Africa, in my personal view, is the world's most fascinating region; it includes Zimbabwe and Zambia with their Victoria Falls and huge variety of wildlife; Botswana with the world's biggest inland delta, the Okavango; Namibia, which, apart from its wildlife, has one of the world's most beautiful living deserts and is uniquely dramatic in its scenery, and South Africa with its grand mountains, its beautiful coastline, and its variety of protected areas, its unparalleled flora and unequalled variety of wildlife.

East Africa is also ready for a renaissance – as a region. Few people book just to visit, say, Uganda, beautiful though it is. But they do book to go to "East Africa" with Kenya's Maasai Mara Game Reserve, Mount Kenya and the Great Rift Valley; Tanzania's snow-capped Kilimanjaro, Ngorongoro Crater's spectacular wildlife and the Serengeti; Uganda's gorillas; and Rwanda's lakes, gorillas and chimps.

FOOTNOTE

I have been deliberately ambivalent about the modern, fairly disciplined professional hunting industry, beyond commenting on the shameful canned hunting sector, whose only appeal is to the dregs of the hunting fraternity. My ambivalence is mainly because I can see that ethical hunting has its uses; it has its code and it can be controlled. In the eyes of many, however, it remains an unsavoury sport.

Perhaps Axel Munthe, in his book *The Story of San Michele*, was right: "The time will come when they will cease to sneer, when they will understand that the animal world was placed … under our protection and not at our mercy; that animals have as much right to live as we have, and that our right to take their lives is strictly limited to our right of defence and our right of existence. The time will come when the mere pleasure of killing will die out in man.

"As long as it is there, man has no claim to call himself civilised, he is a mere barbarian – a missing link between his wild ancestors and the man of the future."

POSTSCRIPT

This book was written as Africa's wildlife slaughter crisis appears to be reaching a climax.

China, the major culprit in the 21st century slaughter, announced moves to curb illicit ivory and rhino horn trading. Vietnam, notorious for its role in the slaughter, claimed to have confiscated crates of ivory entering Vietnam but remained silent about the kingpins who openly trade ivory and horn obtained from African poachers sponsored and armed by Vietnamese syndicates. Meanwhile, the American-based Elephant Action League reported in July 2017 that there was no sign of China's demand for rhino horn lessening. Vietnam traders told undercover agents that 80% of rhino horn entering Vietnam was bought by China.

Africa stepped up its policy of militarising conservation with Botswana announcing a "shoot to kill" policy. But South Africa's Minster of Environment, Edna Molewa, shocked conservationists worldwide by announcing she would allow lion bones to be exported to the Far East by lion breeders. The powdered bones fetch high prices for blending with spurious "tonic" wine. She further announced – without divulging what research, if any, was behind it – that rhino horn from privately owned stockpiles could be traded within South Africa (where there is no demand) but cannot be exported until she gives permission.

In mid-2017 a best-selling book in Kenya, *The Big Conservation Lie*, by journalist John Mbaria and zoologist Dr Mordecai Ogada, castigated the media, especially TV, for wilfully portraying conservation heroes as being exclusively white while blacks are portrayed as poachers, squatters or, at best, indifferent to conservation. The book blamed whites for the slaughter of colonial times and said many current and famous conservation "heroes" hunted for fun and supported the hunting safari industry.

Index